The Pause

The
Pause

●

Experiencing
Time
Interrupted

JULIAN JASON HALADYN

McGill-Queen's University Press

Montreal & Kingston • London • Chicago

© McGill-Queen's University Press 2024

ISBN 978-0-2280-2080-6 (cloth)
ISBN 978-0-2280-2081-3 (paper)
ISBN 978-0-2280-2082-0 (ePDF)
ISBN 978-0-2280-2083-7 (ePUB)

Legal deposit second quarter 2024
Bibliothèque nationale du Québec

Printed in Canada on acid-free paper that is 100% ancient forest free (100% post-consumer recycled), processed chlorine free

This book has been published with the help of a grant from the Canadian Federation for the Humanities and Social Sciences, through the Awards to Scholarly Publications Program, using funds provided by the Social Sciences and Humanities Research Council of Canada.

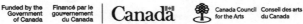

We acknowledge the support of the Canada Council for the Arts. Nous remercions le Conseil des arts du Canada de son soutien.

McGill-Queen's University Press in Montreal is on land which long served as a site of meeting and exchange amongst Indigenous Peoples, including the Haudenosaunee and Anishinabeg nations. In Kingston it is situated on the territory of the Haudenosaunee and Anishinaabek. We acknowledge and thank the diverse Indigenous Peoples whose footsteps have marked these territories on which peoples of the world now gather.

Library and Archives Canada Cataloguing in Publication

Title: The pause : experiencing time interrupted / Julian Jason Haladyn.
Names: Haladyn, Julian Jason, author.
Description: Includes bibliographical references and index.
Identifiers: Canadiana (print) 20230592589 | Canadiana (ebook) 20230592597 | ISBN 9780228020806 (cloth) | ISBN 9780228020813 (paper) | ISBN 9780228020820 (ePDF) | ISBN 9780228020837 (ePUB)
Subjects: LCSH: COVID-19 Pandemic, 2020—Psychological aspects. | LCSH: COVID-19 Pandemic, 2020—Social aspects. | LCSH: COVID-19 Pandemic, 2020—Political aspects.
Classification: LCC RA644.C67 H346 2024 | DDC 362.1962/4144—dc23

For Miriam
Look out! Another paused mushroom

Contents

Figures | ix

Preface | xi

Acknowledgments | xvii

Covid-19 and the Crisis of Imagination | 3

Air | 21

Pause and Effect | 42

Seeing the Virus | 64

A Theory of Social Distancing | 86

Asynchronicity | 109

On Abstraction, Boredom, and Pausing | 129

Notes | 149

Index | 171

Figures

"This is fine" toilet paper in Covid-19 meme. | xv

Installation view of Serkan Özkaya and Joseph Beuys, *Left Is Right, Down Is Up* at Postmasters Gallery, New York, 2020. Image courtesy of the artist. | 4

Installation view of Serkan Özkaya and Joseph Beuys, *Left Is Right, Down Is Up* at Postmasters Gallery, New York, 2020. Image courtesy of the artist. | 5

"Concerning Masks," cartoon by Tooke, *Calgary Daily Herald*, 26 October 1918. Public domain. | 25

Deer in the streets of Junin de los Andes in Patagonia, Argentina, 2020. | 37

CDC illustration of the "golf-tee-shaped" spikes of the SARS-CoV-2 virus, created in 2020. Public domain. | 57

Transmission electron microscope image of SARS-CoV-2, captured and colourized at NIAID's Rocky Mountain Laboratories in Hamilton, Montana. Credit: NIAID (CC BY 2.0). | 58

FIGURES

Telephone operators in High River, Alberta, during the
Spanish flu pandemic of 1918. Glenbow Archives, Archives
and Special Collections, University of Calgary. Public
domain. | 73

Letter carrier in New York wearing mask for protection
against influenza. New York City, 16 October 1918. Public
domain. | 75

Self-portrait with *Bob's Burgers* mask. | 77

Social distancing sign, Toronto 2022. Image courtesy of
Kashfia Arif. | 89

Covid-19 vaccine bottles. Image courtesy of Kimberly
Haladyn. | 99

"Does everyone understand?" teaching with Zoom meme. |
121

Yam Lau, *Covid Life* (still), 2022. Image courtesy of the artist.
| 131

Robert Fitterman in *Left Is Right, Down Is Up* at Postmasters
Gallery, 11 July 2020. Image courtesy of Robert Fitterman. |
137

Robot tour of Hastings Contemporary, April 2020.
© Courtesy of Hastings Contemporary. | 139

Preface

Pause.
— Georges Perec[1]

"Will 2023 Be the Year Covid-19 Becomes Endemic in Canada?" asks the title of journalist Teresa Wright's article published on 1 January 2023. As uncertainty around the pandemic continued, especially in light of China's abandoning of its zero-Covid policy in late 2022 – which suddenly exposed millions of people to the virus – it was curious to start off a new year by questioning the term we use to describe the state of Covid: *pandemic* or *endemic*. As Wright notes, "declaring or deciding that a virus is endemic is not a straightforward or clearly-defined practice."[2] To make such a declaration is to officially claim that this novel coronavirus is no longer an acute or immediate crisis, but instead has now become a long-term or chronic problem. At what point do a virus and its effects become something we just have to "live with"? And what separates this pandemic status, which was also "not a straightforward" decision, from being characterized as endemic? We might even ask, how much of such a distinction is *imaginary*? Infectious disease specialist Dr Isaac Bogoch goes so far as to say that a lot of making this decision "is based on politics, on perception,

PREFACE

and different places might come up with different definitions."[3] Yet my main purpose is to decide how Covid-19 exists in relation to the world and whether its effects on humanity are temporally containable or will continue to persist in some form or other over a longer period.

Imagining the temporality of a pandemic is difficult if not impossible, especially from inside the event. With changes in the contagion and how it affects individuals and societies, the way we experience time also changes, often quite radically. The sense of time one experiences while witnessing the end *but not the end* of the pandemic, as the world wanted to believe in early 2023, is not the same as that experienced in lockdown, when one is closed off from the world in a contained environment (whatever that looks like for a given individual). I feel that one particular notion of time defines the unique situation of living inside a pandemic: that of *the pause*. Here time is not continuous but moves through fits and starts; one experiences moments of hesitation when life quite literally feels as if it has been paused, not moving forward and therefore somehow outside of the "normal" progression of life. As defined throughout this book, *the pause* is not an absolute condition but, like the time of pandemic itself, one that changes from moment to moment and must be approached in its simultaneity.

Given that my own experience is necessarily part of this investigation of *the pause*, I feel it is important to share the process I went through in writing this book. Entering the first lockdown in March 2020, my partner, Miriam Jordan, challenged me to write a book. I assume this was out of concern

PREFACE

that I would not respond well to being confined for such a long period. Giving me a new project would act as the perfect distraction – and it obviously worked. While I did not start out with a plan to write on the Covid-19 pandemic, I became increasingly fascinated by the events unfolding in relation to the virus and decided to try and capture some of the experiences.

This desire was shared by many people at that time, with innumerable accounts and analyses and testimonials being made public in the early months. Most notably, it seemed as if every major critical thinker in the world felt an immediate obligation to say something about the pandemic, either by sharing observations or by critiquing early responses to dealing with the contagion, or both. What I found interesting about these responses was how many of them directly reflected the main ideas and themes their authors had previously written on; we might say there was a mirror effect that allowed them to see their own perspectives and theories in and through the virus. For example, Giorgio Agamben saw the *state of exception*, Judith Butler the *limits of capitalism*, Naomi Klein her ideas of *disaster capitalism*, Byung-Chul Han questions of *digital surveillance*, Slavoj Žižek a form of *communism* (a common "utopic" reading), Jean-Luc Nancy a *communovirus* – I could go on. And I do not deny that I too have imagined a pandemic that suspiciously parallels ideas that I explore in my own research, such as the consideration of boredom in the last chapter.

When I began, my writing was quite general, driven by an attempt to capture the details of the moment, with an overarching aim of documenting the (somewhat) unique experience

xiii

PREFACE

of being inside a pandemic. Too many of the other texts I was reading seemed to assume the end of the contagion from the outset, with few honestly considering the reality of what was actually happening in the world. The idea of *the pause* emerged as a way to confront this presentness of the virus and its effects, not as a means to a "post-Covid" end, but instead as a question of human life and existence. What does it mean to "pause" life? Were we – are we – in fact "paused" as we live through Covid-19 and its effects? Before long, the entire book became about this term, considering different aspects and experiences of the pause, from gallery exhibitions to NHL games, from the closing of stores and restaurants to the necessary stoppages in the lives of individuals. The most profound state of pausing was the lockdown, when people's lives quite literally were put on hold and felt that way. *The Pause* became a chronicle of thinking through this state of pausing, what it meant and how it changed. It was tied to the pandemic condition that the world was facing with Covid but also the history of similar existential crises or problems (acute or chronic).

By the end of 2020, the book as I had originally imagined it was largely written in rough form. However, when I started to edit the existing chapters it became obvious that, because of changes in the pandemic, specifically new information on the virus and differences in how individuals and communities were coping with the emergency measures, I was going to have to adjust some of what I wrote. In the worst cases, parts of my writing had become irrelevant. What seemed significant in one phase of the pandemic – the shortage of toilet paper

xiv

PREFACE

"This is fine" toilet paper in Covid-19 meme.

during and in the aftermath of the early lockdowns for example – became a joke in another; the sheer number of toilet paper memes speaks to both the seriousness and absurdity of this "problem."

All authors writing on the pandemic necessarily had to deal with this issue in some way because of the unpredictability of the virus and the effects it directly and indirectly caused, making it difficult if not impossible to know (assume) what is or will be important. This uncertainty, which got worse through 2021 into 2022, really made the project feel irrelevant in that moment, and forced me to rethink the project. Even the core idea of *the pause* had to be rethought in light of the fact that

PREFACE

"pause," as Peter Conlin nicely worded it in the interview he conducted with me in June 2022, "suggests a relatively short period of time."[4] Yet in this case the *pausing* continued for some time, changing its meaning throughout the pandemic and becoming something more complex.

The final configuration of this book reflects this rethinking, picturing the Covid-19 pandemic through a layering of different perspectives, which are presented simultaneously. On the one hand, I tried to hold on to experiences from the early pandemic that continued to feel valid, either actually or as a way of capturing a now lost moment. On the other hand, I have attempted to provide a broad range of cultural and temporal perspectives that demonstrate the scope of this pandemic condition. It is within such changing realities that the pause is most visible, as well as meaningful. This book was written over three years of pandemic time and includes elements from various moments along the way, imagining what it means to live a life on pause.

Acknowledgments

Lots of people
– Georges Perec[1]

Writing this short book has proven a lively and challenging undertaking, especially from inside the Covid-19 pandemic. My sincere thanks go to Khadija Coxon of McGill-Queen's University Press, who was a champion of this book at a key moment when I needed it. This book would have been inconceivable without her support.

Parts of the book draw from material that has been presented and published elsewhere in early and somewhat different form: elements of my discussion of Serkan Özkaya's exhibition *Left Is Right, Down Is Up* are derived from my exhibition review published in *Burlington Contemporary* on 5 June 2020; the section titled "Covid-Boredom" in the final chapter is an expanded and reworked version of an article, "Depressed or Bored? How Covid-Boredom Intensifies the Fear of Missing Out," which was published in *The Conversation* on 7 February 2021. I thank the editors of these publications for their help. For "Depressed or Bored?" I also want to thank the dean of my department at

ACKNOWLEDGMENTS

OCAD University, Sarita Srivastava, for her encouragement and help. The sections "Relational Paralysis" and "Empty Spaces of the World" benefited greatly from the presentations of this research at SIP – the Society for Italian Philosophy Fifth International Conference on 11 June 2022 – and on the "Let's Get Digital" panel, chaired by Elyse Longair and Jevi Peters, at the Universities Art Association of Canada Conference on 28 October 2022. Many thanks to those who organized these events, as well as to the individuals who attended and made comments.

Discussion with many friends, family, and colleagues has informed my thinking on the issues addressed here. Thanks especially to André Alexis, Grace An, Kashfia Arif, Maria Belén Ordóñez, Atanas Bozdarov, Keith Bresnahan, Peter Conlin, Bronte Cronsberry, Emily Dickson, Robert Fitterman, Michael E. Gardiner, Alberto Gomez, Janice Gurney, Andy Haladyn, Kimberly Haladyn, Susan Haladyn, Maxwell Hyett, Miriam Jordan, Shelley Kopp, Yam Lau, Elizabeth Legge, Madeline Lennon, Elyse Longair, Liane McCulloch, Serkan Özkaya, Andy Patton, Jevonne (Jevi) Peters, Heather Robson, Magda Sawon, Leila Talei, Dot Tuer, Émilie (Lili) von Garan, and Maya Wilson-Sánchez. Cynthia Lauer of Plum Publishing Development Services assisted with numerous aspects of publishing this book; this project was supported by the Dean's Publication Grant from the Faculty of Arts & Science at OCAD University.

There is no evidence that Georges Perec, while at one point observing a kind of dachshund, ever went into detail about the inner lives of these hounds. Confined during the Covid-19 lockdowns with Trixie and Teeny, my two dachshunds, their

ACKNOWLEDGMENTS

playful presence, as well as that of my cats, Carlyle and Lars, came to subtly inform this work. Finally, I am especially grateful to Miriam for all her support and continual encouragement throughout the process of realizing this book.

The Pause

Covid-19 and the Crisis of Imagination

Moments of emptiness
– Georges Perec[1]

Experience on Pause

In late February 2020, I received an invitation from the artist Serkan Özkaya to visit his upcoming exhibition *Left Is Right, Down Is Up*, at Postmasters Gallery in New York City. This was an opportunity for me to experience his artwork, *Proletarier Aller Länder* (*Workers of the World*), an installation consisting of a multitude of near-identical small red abstracted foam figures that blanket the floor, requiring anyone who walks into the space to step on them: to watch them collapse under your feet and then to re-form, little hands held high, once released. Photographic and even video documentation cannot properly communicate the experience. In this particular exhibition of the work, the mass of diminutive *proletarier* were serenaded by the voice of iconic modernist artist Joseph Beuys (with two colleagues), a recording from 1968, chanting: *Ja ja ja ja ja, nee nee nee nee nee*. Yet, as it happened, my plans and the opening of the show itself were disrupted by the Covid-19 pandemic.

Above and opposite
Installation view of Serkan Özkaya and Joseph Beuys, *Left Is Right, Down Is Up* at Postmasters Gallery, New York, 2020.

In an email dated 16 March, Serkan wrote to me: "As for my show in NY we didn't really have an opening after I finished installing but kept the gallery open for individual visitors during the first day. Then with Magda [Sawon] we decided to 'freeze' the show until the pandemic is over." As a direct result of the emergency measures put into place to slow the spread of the virus, the restrictions on groups of people gathering, Postmasters Gallery closed its doors to the public for what would end up being months. Even though the exhibition was installed as planned, ready for the opening on 14 March, it was instead "frozen" in the empty gallery. In a press release, wonderfully titled "How to Experience 'Experience Art' in a Pandemic – A Modest Proposal," gallery owner Magda Sawon writes: "The exhibition is now on pause, sitting still in a closed gallery."[2]

Pause is one of several terms that have been used to define the temporary interruption of experiences, both actual and possible, that have resulted from Covid-19 and its effects. We

see this in the ways it has been used in various public discourses, for example as an important element within the titles of news and popular media articles. It is worth listing a selection of such titles: "Xi Warns China Can't Stay on Pause for Much Longer" (*Forbes*, February 2020); "Quebec will Be 'On Pause' until May 4, as Covid-19 Cases Still on Rise" (*Montreal Gazette*, April 2020); "Northern Ontario First Nations Want Pause to Mining Permits until Covid-19 Subsides" (*CBC News*, April 2020); "Health Department 'Implores' People to Pause Yard Sales" (*Commonwealth Journal*, June 2020); "Ontario Pausing the Lifting of Capacity Limits in Remaining Settings Where Proof of Vaccination Is Required" (Ontario Government, November 2021); "Why the NHL Hit Pause on the Season Now, and What Comes Next" (*ESPN*, December 2021); "Pandemic Recovery Hits the Pause Button" (*Food Technology Magazine*, February 2022); and "Pride Fest Back in Full Force after Pause due to Covid-19 Pandemic" (*CBS*, June 2022). At its most basic, the pause represents a particular way of understanding time within the pandemic, in which the assumed continuum of life and lived experience, both individual and societal, is unexpectedly disrupted.

For many, it felt as if their lives were paused all at once, suspended in time and space, resuming only bit by bit over what has ended up being years. Through shutdowns, the limits of virtual engagements, and increasing problems with supply chains, among other issues, people around the world have been faced with the task of having to rethink aspects of their lives and work. As chief creative director and founder of JNBY (a global China-based clothing brand) Li Lin states:

Covid-19 and the Crisis of Imagination

The suspension of outdoor activity in China coincided with the Chinese New Year, so all businesses naturally took a pause. The only problem is that the pause was extended considerably. In our case, the autumn and winter shows and orders were all impacted ... When all the smooth running suddenly halted, it seems to be time for our management to give the future of JNBY some serious thought, to see if any changes need to be made, and perhaps to lead to a different future.[3]

This idea of the pause (*perhaps*) leading to a *different future* is a foundational concern when thinking through not, I suspect, just this pandemic but all pandemics due to the extreme uncertainty such events raise. Which causes us to be aware of the limits of our control over our lives, to be painfully conscious of the limits of human experience.

My intention in writing this book is to define what I am calling *the pause*: an experience not of the Covid-19 pandemic itself, but rather its effects on a lived existence that has felt interrupted and without a full sense of presence these weeks, months, years. In the midst of living through the pandemic, a true moment of existential hiatus, we encounter a misrecognition of experience in which the present often feels like an absence – like a memory we are concerned we may have already forgotten. Within a pandemic, human life is caught between potential and its enactment, captured within the very hesitation or refrain that has become our everyday existence, an experience of non-experience that is made apparent in and through the pause. What happens when life itself is paused?

THE PAUSE

Writing in a Time of Contagion

"Being told like the rest of humanity to 'stay at home' because of the pandemic," Catherine Malabou writes in a text on the eighteenth-century philosopher Jean-Jacques Rousseau's discussion of his quarantine during the plague at Messina in 1743, "I immediately remembered this passage from the *Confessions*. While all of his companions of misfortune chose to stay confined together on a boat, Rousseau decided to be locked up in the lazaretto instead." Forced to stop in Genoa on his trip from Paris to Venice, Rousseau was quarantined for twenty-one days in the lazaretto, "a hospital for those affected with contagious diseases," an act that Malabou draws special attention to:

> There is something else perhaps more profound in this passage, which is that quarantine is only tolerable if you quarantine from it – if you quarantine within the quarantine and from it at the same time, so to speak. The lazaretto represents this redoubled quarantine that expresses Rousseau's need to isolate from collective isolation, to create an island (*insula*) within isolation. Such is perhaps the most difficult challenge in a lockdown situation: to clear a space where to be on one's own while already separated from the community.[4]

There is a lesson in Rousseau's choice to self-isolate even within an already existing collective isolation, one that is tied to his act of retrospectively writing about the experience. Quarantine,

8

Covid-19 and the Crisis of Imagination

we might say, is an imposed understanding of space as protective, which in this case defines a space within a space, inside of which the individual can escape the purely protective nature of such self-isolating measures. For Malabou, as she admits later in the text, "writing only became possible when I reached such a confinement within confinement, a place in the place where nobody could enter and that at the same time was the condition for my exchanges with others." Writing functions as a profound ability to *create an island* within the pandemic, to construct another world that one can inhabit at a time when the real world feels uninhabitable.

It is interesting to note that practices of quarantine, which were put into place in early modern culture to help prevent the spread of plague, are tied to a growing belief in contagion. "The notion that plague might be contagious appeared as early as the late fourteenth century," Christian W. McMillen writes in *Pandemics: A Very Short Introduction*.[5] Given the possibility that an illness might be contagious – transmitted through contact – it makes sense to develop strategies to prevent such contacts from occurring – as have been implemented during the current pandemic in the form of social distancing, self-isolation, closing spaces in which people gather in large numbers, restricting travel, and other limitations on individual and collective interactions. Like a "second Robinson Crusoe," we all had to make arrangements for our respective modes of quarantine.[6]

Rousseau's account of the plague at Messina, albeit idiosyncratic, is part of a long history of writing on plagues and pandemics that dates back to antiquity. In *The History of the Peloponnesian War*, ancient Greek historian Thucydides discusses the plague of Athens that began in 430 BCE, resulting in the death of an estimated quarter of the population. He frames his writings on this event by noting: "But I shall simply tell it as it happened, and describe the features of the disease which will give anyone who studies them some prior knowledge to enable recognition should it ever strike again. I myself caught the plague, and witnessed others suffering from it."[7] Here he stresses the role of his own experience in this first-hand account of the events, highlighting the fact that he fell ill and survived this pestilence. Subsequent writers on the plague of Athens draw on Thucydides's history as the basis for their own discussion, including, most notably, the ancient Roman philosopher and poet Lucretius in the final book of *On the Nature of Things*. In this way, writings on plagues are divided into two categories: accounts based on first-hand experience of the events and recountings of past events composed using other sources. This first category is important because such accounts allow us access not just to information *on* a contagion but also to experience *of* a contagion.

The significance of this can be seen in the specific attitude or interest a given writer takes when addressing the events and their position within them. Thucydides emphasizes the fact that he himself *caught the plague* and witnessed its effects, thereby establishing the credibility of his history. Procopius, the Greek historian of late antiquity, writing on the plague of Justinian that began in 541, stresses the unimaginable quality

Covid-19 and the Crisis of Imagination

of the "calamity" – which, he writes, "is quite impossible either to express in words or to conceive in thought any explanation, except indeed to refer it to God."[8] The Renaissance writer and poet Giovanni Boccaccio wrote what has become one of the most famous descriptions of the Black Plague, specifically as it struck Florence in 1348, his account of which begins his book the *Decameron*. In Ethiopia, the fourteenth-century nun St Zena Maryam wrote in her hagiography about her encounter with the Black Plague as a young girl – historians only recently believing that the plague reached sub-Saharan Africa – which killed her mother, was responsible for the death of her brothers, and was the main reason she became a nun.[9] In each of these cases, individual experience serves to ground what is otherwise *quite impossible to express in words*.

Daniel Defoe attempts to share some "observations or memorials" of the seventeenth-century Great Plague of London in *A Journal of the Plague Year*. Though it was at least partially fictionalized, his realistic and detailed account captured the experience so well that the distinguished English physician Richard Mead, in his 1744 book *A Discourse on the Plague*, quoted Defoe's description.[10] It was also during the Great Plague of London that Isaac Newton, forced to leave Cambridge and stay for about two years at his family home in Woolsthorpe, had his *annus mirabilis* or "marvelous year" of discovery. While he does not write about the plague itself, Newton credits the "plague years" with allowing him to make three of his most significant discoveries – on calculus, optics, and gravity. Newton's particular form of quarantine has been much discussed during the current pandemic, especially in the early days, as a model – and sometimes foil – for those who attempted to use this pause as a space to (creatively) work.

Yet, against the backdrop of contagion there is often the opposite situation, when the issues of death and survival eclipse all other concerns. We see this most powerfully in the writing of personal letters, of which I will give two examples. The first is a letter written by Francis Blackman, a First Nations resident of the Ottawa reservation in Peshawbestown (Michigan), addressed to George Lee of the Mackinac Office of Indian Affairs on 9 November 1881. Blackman begins with the direct statement: "We have a terrible sickness here at this place."[11] The sickness was smallpox, brought to the Americas by European settlers, infecting the Indigenous populations starting in the sixteenth century and continuing into the nineteenth century, with catastrophic loss of life and unimaginable cultural consequences. Blackman's letter was a personal appeal for help from a community that was overwhelmed by illness. The second is a letter by Lutiant LaVoye (alternatively Van Wert), a nineteen-year-old Ojibwe woman who was a volunteer nurse in Washington (DC) during the Spanish influenza, or flu, epidemic of 1918, written to her friend Louise. In it, Lutiant – as she signs her letter – at one point tells of the death of four officers in her charge: "I was right in the wards alone with them each time, and Oh! The first one that died sure unnerved me – I had to go to the nurses' quarters and cry it out. The other three were not so bad. Really, Louise, Orderlies carried the dead soldiers out on stretchers at the rate of two every three hours for the

Covid-19 and the Crisis of Imagination

first two days they were there."[12] Her struggle to put this experience into words is palpable and gives a sense of the human limits of comprehending the realities of a world that feels physically and psychologically uninhabitable.

Inside the Pandemic

Writings on Covid-19 and its extended effects started to appear almost from the outset and continued virtually unabated throughout the pandemic. From celebrated Chinese writer Fang Fang's diary entries on the social media platform Sina Weibo that started on 25 January to Italian philosopher Giorgio Agamben's controversial article in the newspaper *Il Manifesto* on 26 February, we have seen an imminent need to address – and continually re-address – the situation at hand. As Alexandra Alter writes in her *New York Times* article of May 2020:

> Three months into the biggest public health and economic crisis of our era, authors and publishers are racing to produce timely accounts of the coronavirus outbreak, with works that range from reported narratives about the science of pandemics and autobiographical accounts of being quarantined, to spiritual guides on coping with grief and loss, to a book about the ethical and philosophical quandaries raised by the pandemic, written by the Slovenian philosopher Slavoj Žižek.[13]

THE PAUSE

The World Health Organization (WHO) declared the novel coronavirus a global pandemic on 11 March and Žižek's *Pandemic! Covid-19 Shakes the World* was in print by May, seemingly in an attempt to be the first book on this event. Such urgency, sometimes to the point of excess – the final chapter of Žižek's book was emailed to me and is not in the physical copy I own – is symptomatic of the early stages of the pause.

The fact that this is the first major global pandemic to take place in the age of social media, a form of communication that privileges immediacy and a reliance on individual opinions, beliefs, and interests, helps explain the accelerated need to respond. In their introduction to the special issue of *Topia: Canadian Journal of Cultural Studies* dated 23 March, editors Penelope Ironstone and Greg Bird outline the process of this "rapid response collection of essays," in which authors were contacted on 15 March and asked to submit their final texts by 20 March; the "point of this exercise was to provide alternative perspectives on what is unfolding and to do so while early in the throes of an unfolding pandemic. We were writing in the midst of the event itself."[14] (It is worth noting that when I accessed this collection on 29 June 2022, a number of these texts had been removed.) Given how rapidly these essays were researched and written, it is no surprise that the overall tone of the collection was quite personal. One essay by art historian John Paul Ricco includes an introductory note in which the author admits: "This writing has been a blessing, warding off feelings of anxiety that hover around the edges of my days, and that strike each time I pay attention to the 'news.' Perhaps they will offer something of the same to readers."[15]

14

Covid-19 and the Crisis of Imagination

Given the "novelty" of this particular coronavirus, most notably that it is happening to us, that people around the globe all have to deal with it in some manner, we witness an intense desire to express and experience others' expressions on this experience – again, with a sense of urgency. In their own ways and from their own perspectives, authors have been attempting to make sense of a situation that has changed dramatically over its duration. On the one hand, the desire to express has pushed people to document what is for most of us a unique moment in life as it unfolds. Similar to the historical accounts discussed above, first-hand narratives give us a personal glimpse into the realities of a crisis that we see through the eyes of people who are experiencing it, from any number of perspectives. On the other hand, (too) many of these expressions are merely individual opinions and beliefs presented as if they are historical facts, substituting personal observations for knowledge on a topic. And the difference between these two poles is not always apparent, especially from inside the experience.

In terms of first-hand accounts, the diary entries of Fang Fang are among the most important early writings on the pandemic. Between 25 January and 8 April 2020, she made sixty posts, all of which were written while the author was in a city-wide lockdown – the collection, which she never imagined would be "published overseas so quickly," was released in eBook form on 15 May. Near the end of her first entry, Fang Fang notes that, by "writing about what is happening," it will "be a way for people to understand what is really going on here on the ground in Wuhan."[16] This desire to communicate her lived experience during the early days of Covid-19, when there was little information about the virus and people were quite anxious about the situation, provided some comfort at the time – "So many people have told me that they could only finally get to sleep after reading my entry for the day" – but also captured details of a moment that now feels quite far away. While her observations are mostly mundane – "I'd like to say a little bit about Mayor Zhou Xianwang's hat," she writes on 28 January – the overall record of her perceptions and activities helps us imagine the realities of this moment in China. The importance of attempting to put such perspectives into words is rarely, if ever, apparent at the time they occur. However, after the time passes, it is almost impossible to reimagine them. Fang Fang's skill as a writer stems from her ability to exist inside what was (is) an unreal situation, to imagine this *pause* in life, and for this reason she was an important resource for my understanding of the pandemic.

It is precisely Agamben's inability to accept that he is inside the pandemic that is on display in his numerous responses, the most significant of which date from 26 February to 23 November 2020. He begins his initial essay, tellingly titled "The Invention of an Epidemic," with the following statement: "In order to make sense of the frantic, irrational, and absolutely unwarranted emergency measures adopted for a supposed epidemic of coronavirus, we must begin from the declaration of the Italian National Research Council (NRC), according to which 'there is no SARS-CoV2 epidemic in Italy.'" The sentiment of his text is immediately evident: the global response has been and continues to be an overreaction, with restrictions placed upon people that are "disproportionate to the threat."[17] On the

Covid-19 and the Crisis of Imagination

day Agamben's essay was published, a reported 374 people were infected with coronavirus in Italy, a number that would increase to an estimated 2,706 infected and 107 deaths by 4 March 2020. One might assume that by April or May he would have rethought his perspective and recognized that the restrictive measures were in fact proportional to the now obvious threat of the virus. An assumption proven wrong by Agamben's continual denouncements and the publication of a collection of these writings in July, with an enlarged edition in August 2021. In the foreword for his book, as published in the English translation, he describes the situation as "the so-called 'pandemic.'"[18]

"The millionth person in the United States died of Covid-19 this month; the global toll has reached almost 6.3 million," Scott McLemee writes in his May 2022 article looking at upcoming books from university presses.[19] Such a qualification, which frames the new titles that address the pandemic – including Alex Jahangir's *Hot Spot: A Doctor's Diary from the Pandemic*, Judith Butler's *What World Is This? A Pandemic Phenomenology*, and Alice Kaplan and Laura Marris's *States of Plague: Reading Albert Camus in a Pandemic* – serves as a brief reminder of the real mortal danger posed by the virus. Yet, while the statistical information above does give the topic a sense of importance, these numbers are mere abstractions that point toward an experience of death that is, in many ways, unimaginable. We can imagine a world without specific individuals who we know, whose absence we are able to feel and understand. But can any of us honestly imagine the world generally without 6.3 million people? To borrow Procopius's phrasing, it is *quite impossible either to express in words or to conceive in thought any explanation, except indeed to refer to statistics.* But being inside the pandemic – being in the pause – means not having the distance necessary to fully abstract experience, to write it as history. Instead, writing from inside the pause means trying to articulate the restlessness of a world that is without a proper grounding.

Imagining the Pause

In Albert Camus's account of a fictional plague that befalls the Algerian city of Oran, wittily dated to 194-, the main character, Dr Bernard Rieux, originally experiences the danger of this contagion as "unreal."

> In his mind, he tried to gather what he knew of this illness. Figures floated in his memory, and he told himself that the thirty great plagues of history had produced close to a hundred million dead. But what were a hundred million dead? … And since a dead man carries no weight unless you've seen him dead, a hundred million corpses strewn across history are nothing but smoke in the imagination.[20]

This discussion of the limits of imagination is followed by a recollection of Procopius's account of the plague of Justinian (Constantinople), which, while brief, gives us a sense of the larger questions being confronted in *The Plague*. Camus situates his imaginary plague within a history of real plagues,

Covid-19 and the Crisis of Imagination

constructing a first-person narrative that functions through historical methodologies that turn the unreal into a "reality." It is curious, therefore, that the narrator of this history is never (overtly) identified; Camus instead allows the plague itself to tell the story through its effects, which are recounted by this unknown narrator, who is positioned to merely tell us "This happened."[21] Putting aside the potential allegory, the book tells us about the logic of documenting what happens inside an experience of contagion – a key reason why Camus's narrative became a touchstone for my discussions of *the pause*.

Camus's way of writing about the idea of *plague*, from outlining documents used in its historicization (testimonies, confidences, and written texts that happened to be acquired)[22] to breaking the story into a series of experiential parts, functions as a guide for generally thinking through a pandemic – aided by the fact that the plague is never (overtly) identified. Which explains the increased interest in the novel almost immediately following the global outbreak of Covid-19. As the title of one article from March 2020 declares: "Albert Camus Novel *The Plague* Leads Surge of Pestilence Fiction." Alongside this *surge* in sales, we also see more people writing about the book using direct references to the current pandemic, with titles such as "What Camus's *The Plague* Can Teach Us about the Covid-19 Pandemic" (2020), "A Mirror in Fiction: Drawing Parallelisms between Camus's *La Peste* and Covid-19" (2021), and, as mentioned above, *States of Plague: Reading Albert Camus in a Pandemic* (2022). In the latter, Alice Kaplan writes: "I joke with Laura that after being sick, I'll never write about Camus's novel the same way."[23] The story that Camus tells clearly speaks to us

THE PAUSE

in this moment, giving us a way to begin to imagine what has happened to us over the past years.

We do not necessarily think about the role of imagination when discussing the Covid-19 pandemic, yet that is precisely what is required to begin to make sense of it. This includes the ways the pandemic has been imagined by individuals, by communities, and through the media – the "documents" that will be used in its historicization. Yet, it must also include those unimaginable qualities and experiences that are a vital part of this reality, and which define the parameters of the pause. I am reminded of Jacqueline Rose's discussion of *The Plague*, where she draws attention to the fact that the death of citizens in the novel "does not speak to the public imagination," quoting Camus from his composition notebook of 1938: "[T]he plague was unimaginable, or rather it was being imagined in the wrong way."[24] The more the pandemic challenges the limits of people's imagination, asking us to live in a world that does not conform with what we think of as "reality," the more fully it becomes *unimaginable*. The quality of writing about the pandemic while living self-consciously inside its effects is of particular significance to me, calling attention to the vital and dynamic nature of an experience that, throughout history, has challenged the limits of human imagination.

Air

Pause.
— Georges Perec[1]

Airing Contagion

On 7 March 2020, the first day of a two-day international symposium on the iconic modern artist Marcel Duchamp that I organized at OCAD University in Toronto, the art historian David Hopkins presented a paper titled "Marcel Duchamp's *50cc of Paris Air*: Dada, Dissemination and Contagion." He discussed the largely overlooked fact that the readymade *Paris Air*, a glass ampoule from a pharmacy in Paris filled with air, was created in 1919 during the Spanish flu outbreak. "The Flu pandemic had ravaged France for the past year. Duchamp asked a pharmacist to empty a small glass filled with medical serum, seal it, thereby refilling it with a substance that must have been utmost on the minds of many of Paris' population at the time, air."[2] Capturing air from Paris, which may have contained the influenza virus, Duchamp then gave this readymade to his friend Walter Arensberg in New York City at a time when the US was contending with its own serious outbreak of the Spanish flu. The artist's choice of the medium of air was, as Hopkins made clear, not a neutral act. While this work has historically been treated almost exclusively in terms of its conceptual properties, with only passing reference to the contemporaneous pandemic and its effects, the idea that the air of *Paris Air* was possibly infected felt very real within the context of the novel coronavirus.

As defined by the Centers for Disease Control and Prevention (CDC), Covid-19 causes a wide range of respiratory and vascular symptoms that can be experienced as either mild or severe illness. Among the ones listed, "shortness of breath or difficulty breathing" has become the symptom most associated with the virus. Also mentioned are emergency warning signs: "trouble breathing, persistent pain or pressure in the chest, new confusion, inability to wake or stay awake, bluish lips or face."[3] The Mayo Clinic lists the following as the most common signs and symptoms of infection: fever, cough, and tiredness.[4] In the weeks leading up to the symposium, there were massive increases in infections and reported deaths due to Covid-19, with governments taking preventive measures to stop its spread, including issuing travel advisories. On 4 March, the WHO estimated that globally 93,090 people were infected and 3,198 dead. This meant that Covid-19 had met two out of the three criteria needed to be designated as a pandemic, the final one being the worldwide spread of the virus. Questioning the delay in using the "p-word," journalist Debora Mackenzie wrote on 26 February: "The virus is now in 38 countries – and counting – on nearly all continents, and those are just the ones we know about. How much more worldwide does it need to be?"[5] The

Air

fact that my Duchamp symposium took place, that all international participants attended and returned home without incident, was quite fortuitous given that all the universities in Toronto ceased in-person activities five days later, on 13 March.

Regardless of the fact that Hopkins had chosen the topic of his paper over a year or so before, a fact he mentioned repeatedly when answering questions after his presentation, it seemed impossible for people listening not to read meaning into the appositeness of his topic. He was talking about contagion at the precise moment when contagion was literally and figuratively in the air. We were thinking through the idea of making art within a pandemic just as the current pandemic was emerging as a worldwide phenomenon. This happy accident – as Duchamp would have called it – did not just make the connection between *Paris Air* and the Spanish flu more apparent, it allowed us to imagine infected air at a bodily level.

Experiential Conclusions

Comparisons between Covid-19 and the Spanish flu have been plentiful throughout the present crisis. This has taken place at various levels of the discourse on the pandemic, from medical studies and academic papers to popular stories and social media posts. If we look at the titles of news stories from one popular media source, the Canadian network Global News, we can see how this comparison has changed over two-plus years: "Over a Century Later, Spanish Flu Bears Some Similarities to Covid-19 Pandemic" (March 2020), "Covid-19 Has Killed as

Many Americans as the Spanish Flu" (September 2021), "'Far from Over': What Past Pandemics Can Tell Us about Ending Covid-19" (March 2022). In the latter, Toronto-based journalist Saba Aziz takes a look at "some past pandemics – recent and old – and how they ended," beginning with the Spanish flu, in an attempt to explore the lingering questions on the end of our current pandemic.[6] To state this in general terms, we look to the past to try to answer questions that are unanswerable in the present.

One of the main reasons for comparing Covid-19 and the Spanish flu is the fact that they are considered the two deadliest pandemics of the modern age. While caused by different viruses, they share many of the same symptoms and are both categorized as contagious respiratory illnesses. It is during the 1918 influenza outbreak that we first see the use of mask mandates that, similar to responses during the Covid-19 pandemic, were met with resistance; a cartoon published in the 26 October 1918 issue of the Calgary *Herald* shows a series of scenes mocking the wearing of masks, which, funnily enough, could have been printed in 2021 and appeared quite contemporary.

It therefore makes sense to think about the current pandemic through the Spanish flu, which has obvious similarities and is also a historically "known" experience. Such an approach helps avoid the difficulties of dealing directly with the unknowns that have dominated various aspects of life throughout this crisis. As the Johannesburg-based novelist Fred Khumalo writes: "People have been asking those of us who are storytellers to write about Covid-19. It's a tall order. You can't write about that which you don't understand. We can compare it to

Air

"Concerning Masks," cartoon by Tooke,
Calgary Daily Herald, 26 October 1918.

the Spanish flu, the Black Death or any of the memorable pandemics of the modern age. But it is not the same. It is still too big to fully wrap our heads around it."[7]

It is worth noting that the same thing was said during the time of the Spanish flu, which spread across the globe killing a reported 50 million or more people; "[T]he *British Medical Journal* wrote in April 1919 that in Bombay influenza 'caused a havoc to which the Black Death ... alone affords a parallel.'"[8] Such a comparison to the Black Plague served to make the Spanish flu feel "knowable." When inside such a crisis, which is composed of so many unknowns and unimaginables, there is comfort in the knowledge of something similar that can be used to help make sense of a seemingly senseless experience.

25

THE PAUSE

The danger of this is in taking such comparisons too far, assuming too much of an overlap between the two pandemics. The problem is, in the words of the eighteenth-century philosopher David Hume: "From causes, which appear *similar*, we expect similar effects."[9] By recognizing in the history of the Spanish flu *similar* causes and experiences, we begin to expect similar effects in our current experiences within the Covid-19 pandemic. Yet, as Hume makes clear, past experience "can be allowed to give *direct* and *certain* information of these precise objects only, and that precise period of time, which fell under its cognization," cannot "be extended to future times, and to other objects, which for aught we know, may be only in appearance similar."[10] In other words, the Spanish flu only provides *direct* and *certain* information on the Spanish flu itself, and cannot be extended to a future pandemic. While it may be helpful to use the history of the Spanish flu to generally think through Covid-19 and its effects, we cannot allow this comparison to prevent us from seeing what is actually happening now.

The problem remains, to use Khumalo's phrasing, that the pandemic is *too big to fully wrap our heads around*. To clarify this position, Khumalo refers to an African proverb: "If you're standing too close to the elephant, you can't see it. All you can see is the shrivelled piece of skin that is right in front of you. To see the elephant in its entirety, and appreciate it for what it is, you need to stand back. You need distance."[11] We have that distance when discussing the Spanish flu, which is now an historically contained event, but we are too close to the Covid-19 pandemic and therefore do not have the distance necessary to

Air

actually *see it*. Instead, as evidenced by the mass of writings that have accumulated since 2020, all we can do is document and describe specific qualities and details of the experience – consistently reminding ourselves not to mistake these for an expression or understanding of the pandemic in its entirety.

Universal Right to Breathe

At its most basic, the act of breathing consists of the body inhaling air, which is taken into the lungs where oxygen is processed – a pause – and then exhaling carbon dioxide back into the air – pausing again. When performing it normally, most beings (humans as well as other-than-humans who breathe in this way) are unaware of this process, which simply takes place, without us realizing it. Only when there is a problem do we typically notice this act, when breathing is not natural and instead becomes a conscious (un-natural) activity of the body. With SARS-CoV-2, the virus infects the lungs, making it difficult to breathe, which in serious cases requires patients to be put onto a ventilator to help them breathe. Introducing her paper "Covid and Camus," Elisabeth Stelson describes how the illness affected her: "I experienced noticeable difficulty breathing, which led me to seek hospital care. A heavy, bone-aching constriction of my chest soon followed along with a fatigue that refused to lift even months later."[12] Such accounts were common, especially in the first two years of the pandemic, before vaccinations were widely implemented, as well as in what is

THE PAUSE

called long Covid, with individuals trying to communicate their now hyperconscious (at times hyperventilating) relation to breathing.

Returning briefly to Duchamp, it is interesting to consider his famous declaration that he preferred breathing over working in this context. This was his way of de-privileging productivity, which undermines the main "value" placed on individual life under capitalism by positioning everyone to be consumers. Instead of being a producer of art, Duchamp wanted to see himself as a *breather* whose life, as much as the objects he created, could be understood as a larger philosophy that speaks to art's role within human life. The idea of "*breathing* here is not just a casual term" for him, Toronto-based artist Yam Lau stated in his talk at the "Duchamp Accelerated" symposium, drawing connections between Duchamp's conception of breathing and mystical ideas of the breath found in many traditions, including Taoism.[13] In this way, the poles are reversed, with people being connected not by working together but rather by simply breathing together.

Such a vision of breathing, while mildly idealistic, does allow us to recognize some of the challenging issues we have faced, directly and indirectly, within this pandemic. Beginning with the fact that, as a viral respiratory illness, the threat and attempted containment of Covid-19 has meant that we must *not* breathe together, given the highly contagious nature of the virus. "Because you breathe all the time," infectious disease researcher Dr Allison McGeer states, "the amount of virus that gets in the air is overwhelmingly greater from you breathing than from coughing or sneezing."[14] While for the most

Air

part this has led people to be cautious and careful, in the best cases respecting the need for distance between them and others, there are those who respond to the breath of others with hysterical repulsion. During the initial year or so of the pandemic, I had innumerable encounters with people who, clearly fearing my presence, even as I respected the suggested social distances, treated me as a mortal threat: violently recoiling, even running away, as if in horror. While this response has been rarer from 2022 onward, there remain those who fear the breath of others. No matter if this is the case or not, breathing together has necessarily become a self-conscious action in this time of contagion.

While vitally connected to the pandemic, historian and political theorist Achille Mbembe locates the act of breathing beyond Covid-19 and its effects into a larger consideration of the threat of *suffocation* in the contemporary world. Reflecting the ideals of the eighteenth-century declaration of universal human rights – inalienable rights that indicated humanity's "emancipation from all tutelage"[15] – Mbembe proposes what he calls the *universal right to breathe*. He writes:

> As that which is both ungrounded and our common ground, the universal right to breath is unquantifiable and cannot be appropriated. From a universal perspective, not only is it the right of every member of humankind, but of all life. It must therefore be understood as a fundamental right to existence. Consequently, it cannot be confiscated and thereby eludes all sovereignty, symbolizing the sovereign principal par

29

excellence. Moreover, it is *an originary right to living* on Earth, a right that belongs to the universal community of earthly inhabitants, human and other.[16]

Thus, in April 2020, when his article was published, in the early stages of the pandemic, Mbembe immediately recognized that the question of breath, brought to the fore by Covid-19, was in fact a nexus point connecting a web of socio-political issues facing contemporary cultures. That the pandemic had, as many other theorists have pointed out in their own ways, simply put pressure on already existing social, political, environmental, and scientific problems. His declaration refuses to limit the question of breathing to Covid-19, or to the human for that matter, instead inviting a *universal* understanding of breathing as a necessity of life.

It is important to situate the pause within this larger perspective, defining it within the pandemic but not limiting the ways in which the pause allows us to recognize issues that are truly important to our lives, to *all life* on the planet. Mbembe's *universal right to breathe* invites us to focus on actual experiences of the ways in which individual beings, both other-than-human and human, are connected by living in a shared world. As a result of the pandemic, specifically the consequences of the emergency measures put into place and related changes in human actions and behaviours, we have had the opportunity to witness the choices we often forget we have. In the first year of the pandemic, two events highlighted key questions of breathing within the pause: the tragic case of George Floyd and what has been called the *anthropause*.

Air

Remembering George Floyd

"Before this virus, humanity was already threatened with suffocation," Mbembe declares.[17] Problems of breath are not new. They are not strictly tied to Covid-19, but instead are part of a larger socio-political problem facing a majority of people in the world, particularly people of colour. While occurring during the pandemic, the death of George Floyd, the forty-six-year-old Black man killed on 25 May 2020 when he was forcibly deprived of oxygen, is the result of continuing systematic racism against Black populations. There are disturbing similarities between his utterance, "I can't breathe," and Eric Garner's in 2014, another Black man killed when a New York City police officer put him in a chokehold until he stopped breathing. Before discussing the concerns for breathing that have been raised by Covid-19, Mbembe wants to make clear that we must recognize the pre-existing threat of suffocation toward which the pandemic has merely drawn more attention.

Arrested on suspicion of attempting to pass a counterfeit bill, Floyd had his hands cuffed behind his back while a police officer knelt on his neck and three other officers stood by as he suffocated to death. Numerous onlookers expressed concern for Floyd, all of which was ignored. In fact, the main reason his death has met with any justice is because of the brave action of Darnella Frazier, the young woman who recorded the event and made it public. As author Jelani Cobb tells us: "The video of Floyd's death is horrific but not surprising; terrible but not unusual, depicting a kind of incident that is periodically re-enacted in the United States. It's both necessary and, at this

THE PAUSE

point, pedestrian to observe that policing in this country is mediated by race."[18] While all officers involved have been found guilty of violating Floyd's civil rights, many advocates have argued that police violence toward Black communities in the US has actually changed little. "For the two-year anniversary, it's woefully underwhelming and not at all something that befits the memory of George Floyd," Black Lives Matter grassroots organizer Melina Abdullah said in response to President Joe Biden's executive order adopting new standards for law enforcement.[19]

Protests in response to Floyd's death began almost immediately. The first were in Minneapolis, where "hundreds of protesters, many wearing face masks to guard against Covid-19, braved the pandemic to protest at the spot where Floyd died."[20] This targeted protest quickly became a national and then, with the help of Black Lives Matter, international call to action against the killing of Black people, as well as more generally a fight against all forms of systemic racism. The anger that Floyd's death caused rang out around the world, inciting people from various global communities to make their voices heard in an attempt to change existing social and political narratives about race.

Yet even the pandemic itself, or, more properly, the response to it by the American government, can be viewed through the lens of racial discrimination. In the words of writer and scholar Melvin L. Rogers:

Amid the revelation that Covid-19 is disproportionately affecting the Black community, we have watched as

Air

states reopen their economies and, so doing, ask that same community to sacrifice even more. Little government attention has been given to the structural inequalities of our health care system and the ways it worsens the pandemic's impact on Black life. The toll of Covid-19 in Black America is not merely the result of a lack of access to good health care, it is also due to the way racial bias structures physician engagement with Black people.[21]

It has even been suggested that the American government's virtual non-action as the numbers of infected and dead continued to rise out of control in (at least) the first years of the pandemic could in part be a response to the fact that Covid-19 disproportionately affects Black and Latinx communities. Cherokee writer and advocate Rebecca Nagle points out that many state health departments in the US, when releasing racial demographic data for 2020, "did not explicitly include Native Americans in their breakdowns and instead categorized them under the label 'other.'"[22] In all of these cases, as with others around the world, vulnerable populations are being put at greater risk during the pandemic as a direct result of existing racist policy and planning.

In their 2022 book *His Name Is George Floyd: One Man's Life and the Struggle for Racial Justice*, journalists Robert Samuels and Toluse Olorunnipa provide an overview not just of Floyd's death but also of his life, as well as the lives of those people affected by him. As they write in the introduction: "Here, we have documented Floyd's struggle to breathe as a Black man in America, a battle that began long before a police officer's knee

33

landed on his neck."[23] The idea of breathing is being used both metaphorically and literally: representing the act of living in the world as a specific body that breathes and the actual prevention of his body from taking air into the lungs to sustain his life. In both cases, there is a problem that requires us to take notice of this typically overlooked bodily act, when breathing cannot be taken for granted and instead must be thought of consciously as part of a fundamental right to existence. Floyd's final words, "I can't breathe," serve as a shameful reminder of violent denials of the (*universal*) right to breathe.

Anthropause

In his text, Mbembe makes a concerted effort to define his ideas about breath as relevant to other-than-humans as much as to the human, going so far as to practically collapse these two categories of life. Through this framework, he reads Covid-19 as "the spectacular expression of the planetary impasse in which humanity finds itself today," raising the question: "Are we capable of rediscovering that each of us belongs to the same species, that we have an indivisible bond with all life?"[24] What the pandemic has generated is a different perspective on existing global environmental issues and problems, the direct result of the significant reduction of human presence and impacts around the globe during the worldwide lockdowns in, most notably, 2020.

This "utopian" moment, as many people have treated it, provided a rare glimpse into how the climate and ecosystems of

Air

Earth might respond to significantly lesser impacts by humanity. Stated differently, we witnessed a brief pause in the anthropocene – our epoch of human-centred engagement with the environment that has resulted in irreversible planetary changes, many catastrophic. For a short time during the early stages of the pandemic, the anthropocene was interrupted or put on pause, suddenly allowing the natural world space and time to exist virtually without humans. Streets appeared to be abandoned, skies and waterways emptied. A group of researchers in 2020 termed this the "anthropause," referring to the "considerable global slowing of modern human activities," which, they note, is "unparalleled in recent history."[25] One of the lead researchers, Christian Rutz, wrote a follow-up article in 2022 in which he described the anthropause as a "substantial reduction in human mobility observed during early Covid-19 lockdowns."[26] For me, the experience of the anthropause captured the unique planetary impasse that humanity has been immersed in for at least the past several decades, demonstrating the effectual truth (Machiavelli) of our current relationship with the environment that sustains all forms of life.

The anthropause was defined mostly through the (seemingly) positive environmental and ecological effects that could be witnessed as a direct result of reductions in human interventions in the natural world. With so many people staying home, toxic emissions decreased significantly, not only from cars but from all forms of transportation; corporate pollution was also reduced, with many industries on hold due to the lockdown measures. One of the repeated examples that showed the visible extent of this change was the popular split-screen image of the India Gate War Memorial in New Delhi, India: foggy and polluted on the left half (October 2019), clear with blue skies on the right half (April 2020). "It is a lockdown silver lining being repeated across the world, as toxic megacities such as Bangkok, Beijing, São Paulo and Bogotá, where varying coronavirus restrictions have been imposed, all reported an unprecedented decline in pollution."[27] In Canada, we saw reduced air pollution in all major urban centres, in June 2020 on average a third of what it had been before the pandemic. This moment, which had many people going so far as to declare that we had solved the environment crisis, was a powerful reminder of nature's ability to recover after only a few months of us *not* polluting.

At times, the ways the Earth became more alive in the absence of excess human presence and interventions felt utopic. Breathing was no longer understood as a human conceit; the *universal right to breathe* encompassed other-than-human beings – including the Covid-19 virus itself – that inhabit the planet with us and we truly came to recognize that fact. One of the key manifestations of this was the visible presence of animals occupying spaces that are, in normal life, dominated by humans. In May 2020, during the anthropause, one could look into the waters in the canals of Venice in Italy and, surprisingly, see "not just a clear view of the sandy bed, but shoals of tiny fish, scuttling crabs and multicoloured plant-life" and at "the Piazzale Roma vaporetto stop, ducks have even made a nest."[28] As Venice began to open back up in June, it was faced with a decision about whether it would return to the "hit-and-run mass tourism on which the economy depends" or, as Mayor

Air

Luigi Brugnaro suggests, allow Venice to be a slow city: "The slowness of Venice is the beauty of Venice."[29] My friends Dot Tuer and Alberto Gomez shared with me an image of deer occupying the streets of Junin de los Andes in Patagonia, Argentina, taken in May during the total shutdown of the country at the beginning of the pandemic – a truly stunning image of a time when, as Dot wrote to me, "the quarantine was magical and accelerated."

Deer in the streets of Junin de los Andes in Patagonia, Argentina, 2020.

Environmentality and Breathing Together

All of these changes produced a very different human world, one that felt like it could see beyond the planetary impasse it had been facing in previous years. In the words of ocean conservation scientist Amanda Bates: "No one can say anymore that we can't change the whole world in a year, because we can. We did."[30] But in truth *we did not*. As was made apparent in 2022, after most restrictions across the globe were lifted, the positive effects of this anthropause proved to be temporary as human life returned to "normal," as human activities and mobility surged – Christian Rutz called this the *anthrosurge*. One example is the phenomenon of "revenge travel," in which we witnessed a huge increase of people travelling "to make up for time and experiences lost to the pandemic."[31] Environmental gains from the pause of the anthropocene were not simply reversed; in many cases they have been made worse.

In fact, it could be argued that the negative environmental effects of the anthropause were there from the beginning, even when they may have appeared to be peripheral. Within months of Covid-19 officially being declared a pandemic, governments around the world began reversing or simply ignoring regulations and initiatives that had been put into place to safeguard the environment. In an article published on 20 May 2020 in the *New York Times*, Nadja Popovich, Livia Albeck-Ripka, and Kendra Pierre-Louis provide a list of environmental rules that had been revised by the American government since the outbreak of the pandemic. Drawing attention to the sheer number of such changes the Trump administration had undertaken in

Air

the last three years, the authors state: "Calling the rules unnecessary and burdensome to the fossil fuel industry and other businesses, his administration has weakened Obama-era limits on planet-warming carbon dioxide emissions from power plants and from cars and trucks, and rolled back many more rules governing clean air, water, and toxic chemicals."[32] The list, divided into six main categories – air pollution and emissions, drilling and extraction, infrastructure and planning, animals, toxic substances, and safety and water pollution, with the additional category "other" – demonstrates the extent of this attack on environmental practices. Governments and corporations used this moment to accomplish what could not easily be accomplished outside such a state of *exception*, changing public policies or allowing illegal activities to take place with impunity because humanity's attentions were otherwise occupied with the crisis of the pandemic.

"I see opportunism fueling illegality as people take advantage of the fragility of the moment we're living, politically as well as economically," director of science at IPAM Amazônia Ane Alencar states: "This coronavirus crisis is turning into an environmental crisis, too."[33] Alencar is specifically addressing the increased razing of the Amazon rainforest that had been subtly, but overtly, supported by the Brazilian government, which made little effort to stop illegal logging and mining during the pandemic. This deforestation also represented an immediate threat to the Indigenous communities who, in addition to being displaced, were at greater risk of being sickened by Covid-19. In the words of Adriano Karipuna, an Indigenous leader in Rondônia: "The dynamic can set in motion a genocide by spreading the coronavirus."[34] As mentioned above, there was concern that these actions were intentional and, like the deliberate infecting of Indigenous peoples in the Americas with smallpox that opened the land to colonization, this disregard for the Indigenous populations was a means of eliminating all factors preventing the financial exploitation of the Amazon and its resources. Like other attempts to undermine environmental practices, which continue to be under siege in numerous countries, it must be remembered that such efforts are not related to Covid-19 but rather serve interests that are clearly exploiting the situation.

Throughout the pandemic, the direct and certain limits imposed on the world by neoliberal capitalist systems and structures have been made (painfully) apparent. These include undermining basic elements that support life, from the life of entire ecosystems to individual life. Feminist theorist Judith Butler points out that something as simple as "stay-at-home" mandates highlights inequalities because "not everyone has a household or a 'family' and increasing numbers of the population in the US are homeless or transient."[35] The events surrounding the death of George Floyd showed the denial of a *fundamental right to existence*, the act of breathing; Mbembe characterizes the threat of suffocation as a war that existed before Covid-19, which is "against everything that condemns the majority of humankind to a premature cessation of breathing, everything that fundamentally attacks the respiratory tract, everything that, in the long reign of capitalism, has constrained entire segments of the world population, entire races, to a difficult, panting breath and life of oppression."[36] Within the

Air

Covid-19 pandemic, this has included the systemic constraints that limit access to health care and other vital resources for Black, Latinx, and Indigenous communities – a blatant inequality repeated in 2022 with a new contagion: to quote the title of one article, "A Repeat of Covid: Data Show Racial Disparities in Monkeypox Response."

A politics of air is predicated on a conscious awareness of the realities that define the planetary impasse that threatens all life on Earth, regardless of the fact that we are living within a pandemic. Similar to other major disruptions in the normalcy of human life, both historical and contemporary, the pause of the anthro*pause* has enacted a moment of (potential) mass retrospection in which we as a species have been given a chance to rethink our understandings of the world and, in Mbembe's words, the *fundamental right to existence*. Instead of trying to make up lost experiences, we might consider recognizing the realities of the pause in the collective act of breathing together, especially at a time when air is utmost on people's minds.

Pause and Effect

> What has changed since yesterday? At first sight,
> it's really the same.
> – Georges Perec[1]

Pause Button

On 12 March 2020, the NHL suspended regular season games due to the evolving situation with Covid-19. As Commissioner Gary Bettman stated in his official announcement, "In light of ongoing developments resulting from the coronavirus, and after consulting with medical experts and convening a conference call of the Board of Governors, the National Hockey League is announcing today that it will pause the 2019–20 season beginning with tonight's games."[2] The day before this decision, it was revealed that a player in the National Basketball Association (NBA) had tested positive for the virus; given the fact that NHL and NBA players share arena facilities, this made it necessary for both leagues to stop playing public games that gather in the range of 20,000 spectators per event. Even when hockey was *un-paused* in late July, the games that started again in August were played in empty arenas until January 2021 when

Pause and Effect

teams in the US began allowing limited fans and in May for Canadian teams.

Colloquially, *pause* describes the temporary delay or hesitation in normal experience that many have encountered, literally and psychologically, throughout the pandemic. In addition to sports being on pause, we saw businesses on pause, jobs on pause, education on pause, travel on pause, weddings on pause, trips on cruise liners on pause, a pause in US funding of the WHO, yard sales on pause, medical treatments on pause, concerts on pause, religious services on pause, a pause in immigrations, art exhibitions on pause, funerals on pause, governments on pause, attempts to pause are themselves paused, and the list continues. This action brings to mind the *pause button* found on remote controls and video and audio interfaces, symbolized by two vertical parallel lines (❙❙), which is used to temporarily halt the play of a broadcast, recording, or stream – as opposed to the stop button, a full square (■), which completely stops play. If, for example, I am watching a movie or streaming a hockey game, I can at any point press the pause button and the video will freeze at that moment, even in mid-action, allowing me to perform other activities and return sometime in the future and, pressing the pause button again, finish watching from where I left off. Used to describe the Covid-19 pandemic, it seems like the idea of pausing allows us to have a comforting conception of "normal" (pre-pandemic) life simply being halted or suspended, assuming things will simply be un-paused at a future date and that "normal" life will continue again precisely where it was when the pandemic paused it.

With the more explicit references to the pause button, we witness the extent to which this logic – the pause as an assumption of control and eventual continuation – serves as a desire to treat pandemic life as an intermission in life, negatively or positively. In the article "Push the Pause Button? Contracts and Covid-19," published in *The National Law Review*, the authors conclude by stating:

> Due to the broad impact, companies need to evaluate whether their contractual performance, or that of their suppliers, has been impacted by Covid-19 and the governmental response to the pandemic. If the parties cannot negotiate a mutually acceptable "pause button" postponing performance, then companies should evaluate whether there are defenses to performance which will reduce or eliminate liability for breach.[3]

The pause button is used metaphorically to give the impression that businesses are not stopping but instead *postponing* their activities and commerce. Pause in this sense is a subtle means of acknowledging things that are no longer being performed or enacted, but with the built-in implication that they will be again in the future. Approached more broadly, the Covid-19 pandemic, Dr Osman Dar claims, "serves as a global pause button, a watershed moment in history for all countries to reflect upon our current state of affairs and consider where they're going and what they might do better. It's an opportunity to make systemic wholesale improvements."[4] Here we witness a widespread belief or hope in the positive potential of pausing;

Pause and Effect

while "normal" life waits for the pandemic to be resolved, we can rethink the *normal* of global life and even take this interval to reimagine the world.

Is this really what we have been dealing with during the pandemic? On the one hand, there is a distinct sense that life was paused in certain respects, mostly connected with general everyday activities and practices that have slowly returned over the years. While it felt for the longest time that eating in a restaurant would never return, in June 2022 not only were most restaurants open but they could also accommodate the same number of people as before the pandemic. On the other hand, there is also a sense that the pause itself has changed and will continue to change life in irreversible ways. For those who want life to return to "normal," this has been deeply concerning; for others who see this as an opportunity to rethink the world – Achille Mbembe's proposal for the *universal right to breathe* is a good example – it has raised hope for the possibility of positive change.

The truth of the matter is that life cannot be put on hold. It continues whether we recognize it or not, whether we accept it or not. While things may have felt as if they were on pause, people necessarily continued to experience the effects of life and lived realities in the world. People missed out on key moments, experiences, and opportunities in their lives during this pandemic that, in a lot of cases, could not be made up after the fact. In this way, the concept of the pause defines the contradictory state in which we find ourselves inside the pandemic: our experience of life on hold is also the reality of our lives continuing, changing, and adapting. Life was never actually paused. What we experience as we wait – whether isolated and social distanced or believing the contagion is over while the numbers of infected increase, as we try to plan and negotiate a future within a time of unknown limitations – is life moving forward in and through a different logic. To help us better understand this logic, let us look more closely at the word "pause."

Pausa / Cessatio

The logic of the pause is grounded in its overdetermined temporality. It announces a time within time, a time embedded in the social and psychological limitations of its own temporal hesitations, a time marked by a multitude of imagined and unimaginable recurrences within everyday lived experience. Understood in its complexity, the pause is concerned with the cause-and-effect relationship of common life in a state of interruption, with activities that were once second nature and could be performed almost without thinking – as discussed in relation to breathing in the previous chapter – suddenly feeling strange, even uncanny. There is a general uncertainty when it comes to the space and time that is the pause, which is rooted in an imposed hiatus or break in the social consciousness (*habitus*) that frames and is framed by individual experience.

The word pause is derived from the Greek *pausis* and Latin *pausa*, generally meaning "stop" or "cessation," describing a temporary delay, or hesitation, or refrain within a process. The ancient Roman philosopher and poet Lucretius employs the Latin term several times in *On the Nature of Things* (*De rerum natura*). In the initial two usages, both in Book 3, Lucretius presents the particular phrase *vitai pausa*, translated as "stoppage of life" by W.H.D. Rouse, "a break in existence" by E.J. Kenney, and "a breach in life" by R.E. Latham. The first passage (I am using Rouse) reads:

> For when you look back upon all the past expanse of measureless time, and think how various are the motions of matter, you may easily come to believe that these same seeds of which now we consist have been often before placed in the same arrangement they now are in. And yet we cannot call that back by memory; for in between has been cast a stoppage of life, and all the motions have wandered and scattered afar from those sensations.[5]

The second passage expands on these ideas: "Death therefore must be thought of much less moment to us, if there can be anything less than what we see to be nothing; for a greater dispersion of the disturbed matter takes place at death, and no one awakens and rises whom the cold stoppage of life has once overtaken."[6] In both, *vitai pausa* describes the state of death in terms of a gap within life, giving an existential reading that locates consciousness or sentience at the core of this *pause*.

It is interesting to note that *pausa* was not a common Latin term, with some commentators observing its colloquial origins. In his commentary on Book 3, Kenney wrote: "After Lucretius, *pausa* disappears from Latin except for an occasional antiquarian revival."[7] Lucretius used this term to qualify particular qualities of life and vitality that, reflecting his over-all investment in a more generalized rather than specific approach, were open to anyone reading his text. We see this in the discussion of the nature of diseases or epidemics that, per-haps oddly, concludes *On the Nature of Things*. A significant portion of this part is a translation or retelling of the ancient Greek historian Thucydides's writings on the plague of Athens, in which Lucretius "cleared away the setting, the unnecessary and the optimistic, leaving a tale of timeless, pointed and unrelieved horror"; by generalizing the account, he positions the reader to (psychologically) fill the picture out for them-selves, "and the result is not Athenians facing the plague but Everyman facing Disease."[8]

Reading Lucretius's writing on plague while living through the current pandemic makes the issues he explored feel quite relevant, even given the over 2,000 years separating *De rerum natura* from the lived realities of Covid-19 and its effects. From his account of the plague in the *baleful* air to the detailed symp-toms of death that mark the illness, from the fearful reactions of the sufferers to their eventual hopelessness and death at the hand of the contagion, from the unburied corpses piled in the streets to the unattended funerals that saw the dead un-mourned, all these very subjective descriptions have parallels in the current day – the differences, in fact, are, in many cases, too slight for comfort.

In a powerful statement, Lucretius explains that the spread of the contagion (*contagio*) infected the neglectful and the careful alike. He writes (I am using Latham): "Without a pause the contagion of the insatiable pestilence laid hold of victim after victim, as though they had been fleecy sheep or horned cattle. One of the main factors that heaped death on death was this."[9] Here Latham translates the Latin word *cessabant*, or *cessation*, as "pause" – Rouse translates it as "cease." Generally meaning "delaying," "omitting," "cessation," or "refrain," *cessation* is used to define through negation the unpausing or unceasing quality of the contagion as, in part, an inner experience. In this context, the term emphasizes the emotional component that individuals bring to their experiences of pandemics, which again is treated as a double negative, with the idea of the pause as an impossible relief.

Feel the Same

"I hope you are keeping well and reasonably sane in this deeply weird time," a colleague wrote to me in an email. Throughout the time of this pandemic, I have sent and received numerous messages that contain similar sentiments, all attempting, one might assume, to acknowledge a powerful overarching feeling of unease that became a shared inner experience of life during the pause. In part, these expressions reflect a genuine concern for the health of people in our lives, an acknowledgment of the seriousness of Covid-19. Another part has to do with putting a voice to the realities of living in these conditions, having to make sense of and personally accept the necessary changes required to function inside the pandemic. In the case of the message above, sent at the beginning of September 2020, it is from a fellow professor who was referring specifically to the strangeness of the fact that the physical university in which we work had closed and, as a result, all our pedagogical and administrative activities had moved online.

On 13 March, it was officially announced that all face-to-face academic and research activities at OCAD University, along with the other universities in Toronto and beyond, were suspended. This included in-person teaching; meetings with students, staff, and faculty; public events, workshops, and other pedagogical gatherings; graduate thesis defences; and exhibitions – any situation where small or large groups of people interacted was no longer permissible due to concerns about spreading the virus. As a result, all teaching moved from in-person to online, a shift that first took place suddenly in the middle of the Winter term immediately following Covid-19 being declared a pandemic. In addition to adjusting to this virtual way of functioning, all educators were forced to rethink how we taught our classes, how we communicated materials to students, what could and could not realistically be taught online, how we plan and organize our classes. Mimicking the form and style of Georges Perec's *The Art of Asking Your Boss for a Raise*, I wrote a humorous account of this question in a text titled "The Art and Craft of Agreeing to Teach Your Course Online."[10] Writer Emily Baron Cadloff described this *big transition* as "an unprecedented educational experiment as faculty attempt to transition their courses *en masse* to online learning."[11] To provide the time and space needed for this shift, OCAD University proclaimed the week of 16 to 20 March as a *pause week*.

What does it mean to have a week that is a "pause"? As a practical gesture, it was a dedicated transitional period that

Pause and Effect

provided individual educators with much-needed time to work out procedures and practices for teaching remotely and navigating the pedagogical realities of this relatively exceptional circumstance. All the usual activities that define life in the university were put on hold in the midst of the term, which for me included figuring out how to deliver the course online, adjusting the parameters of assignments that required in-person interactions, and, likely the most challenging, working with graduate students to figure out how to transform their defences or exhibitions into virtual events. As a conceptual gesture, this pause week was "utopian" in its demarcation of a time and space outside the progression of the semester – a breach of *no-space* in academic life. It was as if the university pushed the pause button and all activities were simply put on hold in mid-motion until the button was pushed again seven days later. In practice, however, this pause was a forced break in the relationship between cause and effect, between the closing of the physical university due to the pandemic and the pedagogical transition in the delivery and organization of teaching. In the end, the pause week was a temporal contradiction, with the present moment being simultaneously postponed and missed, an imagined break that could only in part be an imagined reality.

In an article from 9 April 2020 titled "'This Is Not Going to Be the Same': How University Students Are Coping with Covid-19 Measures," a number of students talked about the changes in their education caused by the pandemic. Emma Zuck, an undergraduate student at Ryerson University (renamed Toronto Metropolitan University in 2022) in Toronto at the time, said: "I think initially when this first happened I was pretty upset and just like, this is not going to be the same."[12] This response reflects a more general societal sentiment of frustration and concern about the effects of pausing so many experiences, most of which, like university education, were being replaced with virtual facsimiles mixed with approximations. Attempting to reimagine the complex universe of the classroom through a digital video platform, a reality that all educators were faced with, is not a matter of transition as much as translation: how do we translate in-person educational experience into an online format? And what is lost in the process? In one of the conversations recorded in his book *The Otherness of the Everyday*, a professor of Chinese art at Birmingham City University, Jiang Jiehong, talked about his experience teaching online in 2020: "I see my students; yet I do not really see them. Some are well prepared, with an appropriate background, real or virtual; some are in a noisy kitchen and some are in their pyjamas; some simply keep their front camera shut."[13] A significant loss of *presence*, the fact of really seeing and experiencing the dynamics of learning.

Digital platforms have been used in many areas of social engagement and entertainment, mostly as a substitute for person-to-person communications and experience. While NHL games were on pause, a multitude of streaming videos allowed us to see and hear from players and coaches, granting us access to personal accounts of their lives during the outbreak. Again, similar to concerns about online education not being *the same*, there were innumerable speculations about how the pause and subsequent restarting of the 2020 season might affect the

Pause and Effect

experience of hockey. Specifically addressing the question of the awarding of the Stanley Cup, Pittsburgh Penguins general manager Jim Rutherford said: "Whoever wins it, it is going to *feel the same* whenever they win it, on whatever day they win it, as it would winning it normally in the middle of June" (emphasis added).[14] While understandable and even necessary, this assumption of *feeling the same* – and its corollary, a fear that it is *not going to be the same* – speaks to a connection between the pause and a desire to define through negation a sense of normalcy within the pandemic. Because the other option is unthinkable.

Enmeshed in this stoppage of life, this break in existence, it is difficult to articulate the exact malaise of this pause in our lives. Even as things cease to *feel the same*, life still remains monotonously the same: bills still need to be paid, dogs need to be walked, the dead need to be buried, and plans for the future thought out (even in the abstract). This *deeply weird time* is tied to the strangeness of the same not being the same, but not exactly different either. Mundane experiences were made to feel off, both common and strange at the same time. I remember looking at Moleskin notebooks before the pandemic, thinking I could get these any time I needed to, only to find myself needing some during the summer 2020 lockdown; out of stock in so many stores, I was forced to order them online, taking whichever type was in stock, and to get them I was required to sit outside the store in the car, waiting, until my order was brought out to me for "curbside pickup." The experience was uncanny, in its more literal German meaning of *unheimlich* or unhomely, the familiar made unfamiliar, yet still familiar at the same time. While I am in no way trying to trivialize the extreme hardships caused by the pandemic, the global loss of life, acknowledging the ways everyday experiences were part of the pause is also important. Pandemics make the world an uncanny place where the same is simultaneously different and still the same.

Narrating Pause through Denial

Within the pause, there has been an obvious hesitation or refrain in recognizing the realities of the Covid-19 pandemic. Pausing here functions as a temporal *no-place* that, to varying degrees in different communities and countries around the world, has allowed humanity to exist in a state of suspended (dis)belief. We see this throughout the pandemic in the extreme suspicion and even denial with which some people treat the seriousness of the virus, which they quickly passed off as an exaggeration on the part of governments, officials, and the media.

Agamben remains a good example of this, not just because of his overall suspicions regarding what he saw as a "disproportionate reaction," but also his more radical statement about "the invention of an epidemic."[15] His denials continued, again manifesting in his outspoken disagreement with the requirements of a green pass in Italy, which went into effect on 23 July 2021 as part of an effort to push people to get vaccinated and allow the country to reopen sooner. In a response published on 26 July, Agamben and Massimo Cacciari begin their joint text with the statement: "The discrimination of a category of

54

people, who automatically become second-class citizens, is in itself a very serious matter, the consequences of which can be dramatic for democratic life. It is being dealt with, with the so-called green pass, with unconscious lightness."[16] A key problem with this argument, as fellow Italian theorist Roberto Esposito succinctly points out, is Agamben's lack of distinction between the *state of exception*, which "arises from the subjective decision of a sovereign will," and the *state of emergency*, which "is an objective necessity, as the great jurist Santi Romano explains well about the earthquake in Messina and Reggio (Italy) in 1909."[17] Those who embrace denial fail to recognize Covid-19 as an emergency situation.

The proliferation of conspiracy theories and "fake news" during the pandemic helps support this position of denial, which, at a crucial stage, was unfortunately fuelled by the then American president and his administration. According to communication theorist and historian David Black: "It's not unfair to say that, whatever one's views on that administration, the president and certain of his senior cabinet officials have promulgated conspiracy theories freely and knowingly, and long before this health crisis."[18] Within the pandemic, such strategies of misinformation have fatal consequences, such as Trump's suggested "cures" for Covid-19, "from antimalarial drugs that he'd seen on Fox to bleach injections" – all while his administration actively disempowered public health agencies, "shunting responsibility to state leaders, and failing to get a handle on the basic information needed to fight the pandemic."[19] Eliot Weinberger, in his article "The American Virus," outlines some of the more outlandish actions and statements of the American president during this time of crisis, as well as related information, such as a list of the statements found on protest signs, including FAKE CRISIS and COVID-19 IS A LIE, protesting the lockdowns in Washington; also noted later in the text are Eric Trump's claims when he was on Fox News that the Democrats were using the pandemic to "prevent his dad from holding rallies and that, after Election Day, 'coronavirus will magically all of a sudden go away and disappear.'"[20] Such examples tell a story that is at odds with the fact that, as of 17 May 2022, the US officially surpassed one million reported Covid-19 deaths.

Narrating Pause through Unimagination

For many, the pandemic cannot properly be understood or imagined as an experience, which is often why we turn to fiction to help us. This is the idea of contagion as *unimaginable* that Camus discussed in *The Plague*. While we may experience the daily disruptions in our lives caused by the virus and attempts to deal with and prevent its spread, and those who contract the illness experience its effects on the body and mind, none of us, not even scientists and medical professionals, can claim to truly experience the Covid-19 pandemic. Because, to use Camus's words, we are imagining the Covid-19 pandemic in the wrong way due to the fact that we "don't think on the right scale for plagues"[21] – a way of thinking that is necessarily beyond the human.

There is an existential conflict that is at the core of humanity's relationship with plagues and pandemics, one defined through an incomplete notion of cause and effect. On the one hand, the effects – protective measures that prevent "normal" life, accepting a state of emergency, recognizing the pandemic logic – are painfully apparent and real, while, on the other hand, the cause – the virus – is just outside people's abilities to properly imagine it into reality. Instead, we conceptually re-imagined the virus as an abstract form that can stand in for the real.

The most obvious way this occurred was how the SARS-CoV-2 virus was pictured. It was often seen in colour representations as spheres with golf-tee-shaped spikes, as opposed to the actual electron microscopy (EM) images that show grey, blob-like abstract shapes with fuzzy edges.

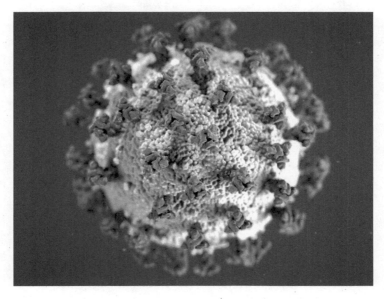

CDC illustration of the "golf-tee-shaped" spikes of the SARS-CoV-2 virus, created in 2020.

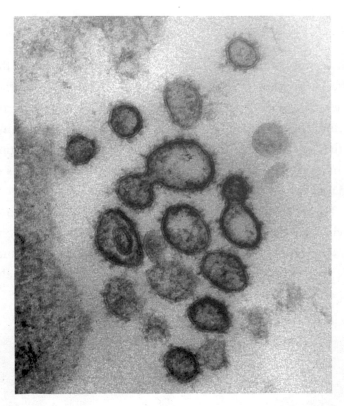

Transmission electron microscope image of SARS-CoV-2, captured and colourized at NIAID's Rocky Mountain Laboratories in Hamilton, Montana.

Viruses do not actually have a colour because they are too small to reflect wavelengths of light; giving the virus colour and recognizable form, as Eva Amsen notes, makes it "more beautiful" and "less threatening" to people, which is why these images are more popular in the media.[22] The abstracting of Covid-19 takes place on various levels of our engagement with the pandemic, from how we imagine its form to the processes we put in place to stop it from spreading, from how we individually navigate the restrictions placed on us to the ways we negotiate the new logics and practices that define our relations with other people, with our work, and with our life. In fact, the core of my own experience is in the constellation of real and imagined encounters, medical and social symptoms that define a state of being while living with a deadly contagion – a perpetual sense of waiting to see what will happen, which is the pause.

In such a narration of this pausing, there is an active disconnect of effect from cause, allowing separation on the level of an individual's inner experience. This can be understood very much in line with David Hume's treatment of causality, especially when he writes: "every effect is a distinct event from its cause."[23] The notion of effects as *distinct events* is strangely appropriate in the current situation. Even while we are able to, for the most part, reconcile missed experiences by simply putting them on pause – like pausing a movie – if each of the direct and indirect effects of Covid-19 are approached as separate events, the result (in true Lucretian style) would be that each individual would have to imaginatively fill out or fulfill this picture of the pandemic for themselves.

Telling Ourselves Stories

Storytelling has always been a way for humans to confront realities without having to directly face the real, which in the case of a plague or pandemic is often overwhelming. It is no surprise therefore that, as novelist Fred Khumalo notes, people have been asking "storytellers to write about Covid-19." He continues: "As much as Covid-19 is scary, it is a worthy challenge to both our medical brethren and our artists. Our imaginative powers are being challenged. We are being stirred from our stupor of complacency, to explore other ways of telling stories, other ways of reaching out to each other as human beings, other ways of being."[24] For Khumalo, the idea of stories as confronting the *challenge* of an event is important, especially, I suspect, when inside the event itself. To this end, various attempts have been made to encourage people to try to be storytellers themselves. One example is the public challenge put out by the global Earth Observation Dashboard in June 2021, in which people were invited, as scientist Anca Anghalae explains, to "tell a visual story about the impacts of the pandemic using Earth observation data and other complementary information such as, for example, mobility, health or statistical data."[25] Through stories, we are trying to capture an experience of life, sometimes personal and other times more historical, inside the pandemic.

We are already witnessing a mass of literature and writing being produced around Covid-19 and its effects that is, in different ways and from different perspectives, attempting to turn the experience of the pandemic into a story. There are important first-hand accounts of living through the crisis, such as Fang Fang's *Wuhan Diary*, in which she brings together a series of her online diary entries documenting the early stages of recognizing the seriousness of the pandemic. In a quote used to describe the book, she states: "The virus is the common en-

60

Pause and Effect

emy of humankind; that is a lesson for all humanity. The only way we can conquer this virus and free ourselves from its grip is for all members of humankind to work together."[26] There are poetic responses, such as the poetry collection *Together in a Sudden Strangeness: America's Poets Respond to the Pandemic*, as well as self-help, medical, economic, and theoretical approaches to understanding different aspects of the crisis. Added to this are the various media and news stories and social media posts, which are in-process cultural narratives that tell us about a desire to locate ourselves as individuals within the pause. Across disciplines, there is a clear push to consider ways to imagine this contagion.

In addition to writings about the present pandemic, historical accounts of past illnesses and crises are also being rethought in light of current experiences. "Ever since the arrival of Covid-19," writes Jacqueline Rose, "sales of Albert Camus's *The Plague*, first published in 1947, have increased exponentially, an upsurge strangely in line with the graphs that daily chart the toll of the sick and the dead."[27] Many commentators have gravitated toward *The Plague* as a way of thinking about and imagining what we are experiencing with Covid-19 – making the unknowable feel knowable, even if both knowledges are fictitious. Similarly, in 2020 there was an increased interest in the Renaissance writer and poet Giovanni Boccaccio's canonical book *Decameron*, a fictional narrative that is set in "the year 1348 when the deadly plague reached the noble city of Florence," a real outbreak of the plague that the author lived through.[28] With titles such as "The *Decameron* – the 14th-Century Italian

Book That Shows Us How to Survive Coronavirus" (*New States-man*, published in March) and "What Would Boccaccio Say about Covid-19?" (*Boston Review*, published in April), there is a clear sense of Boccaccio's book being used to help us find a believable narrative for our current crisis.

The pandemic somehow makes more sense when filtered through a fictional lens, allowing Covid-19 to be read through other imagined experiences. For example, during the early days of the coronavirus outbreak, I was watching the "Plague" episode of the television show *Deadwood* in which the citizens of the fictional encampment of Deadwood face a smallpox outbreak. Initially, it is met with denials and cover-ups, allowing the virus to spread; in response, the main figures within the community put together a plan, isolating the ill out of sight in a pest tent, putting out public notices, and generally communicating the idea that the plague is a passing issue, all in an attempt to control the narrative of events. Watching this during the pause felt both similar and strange; it felt uncanny – as did all popular television shows and movies that dealt with the theme of contagion. The sameness is comforting, allowing us to see our experience from inside an account of dealing with smallpox, a contagion humanity has already (really or fictitiously) survived. But it is also disturbing because, in this case, the same is not actually the same, and we must live through the effects of the *distinct events* of Covid-19. In this way, self-isolating in my home as I watched fictionalized accounts of plagues and pandemics, the sense of sameness haunts me and demands self-conscious reflection.

Pause and Effect

More than likely, we are imagining the current pandemic in the wrong way because we seem unwilling to accept the unimaginable. While many experiences of it are quite mundane or everyday, some of its realities – sudden stoppages of life, the sheer number of deaths, facing our own mortality – challenge and exceed our lived experience. This moment grants us space and time to think – think through the pandemic's effects, direct (bodily) and indirect (socially), think of the unknowability of a situation that seems proximate and distant at the same time. As an event, the pause is the at times minute hesitation or interval separating reality and fiction within the pandemic.

Seeing the Virus

Obvious limits to such an understanding: even when my only
goal is just to observe, I don't see what takes place a few
meters from me.
– Georges Perec[1]

Recognizing/Unrecognizing

Maybe we can learn something about our reactions to the
Covid-19 pandemic from Penelope Ironstone who, in her "The
Pandemic Is (Extra) Ordinary," makes the following statement:

If nothing else, the events of 2020 should give us pause
to consider how pandemics are not merely biomedical
events. Pandemics are simultaneously social, cultural,
economic, and political events with the potential to
occasion rapid, dramatic, and sweeping interventions
into the management, conduct, and understanding
of everyday life.[2]

At the beginning of her essay, Ironstone invites us to consider
the current crisis as a two-part event, the complexities of which
force us to recognize the obvious limitations in our ability to
understand the realities of living in a pandemic. Accompanying

Seeing the Virus

the text is a photograph from 1919 of five women wearing face-masks during the Spanish flu outbreak in Brisbane, Australia. Such images allow us to see the extra-ordinary quality of the moment, the fact that the world is different and people are imagined differently – in this case, the masks signal this distinction. But how do we recognize the extent and limits of these differences in the present, as we are not thinking of but instead living through everyday life?

As a medico-social event, Covid-19 has resulted in the deaths of more than 6,681,000 people worldwide as of January 2023 – requiring a radical reconfiguration of social relations around the world. Attempts at preventing the spread of the virus have caused, in some cases, mass panic and concerns about one's mortality; in other cases, it has caused mass denial and a general refusal to acknowledge the reality of the virus. The biomedical and social aspects of the pandemic have made humanity question itself on a global scale. As an idea, Covid-19 has directly – through contracting the virus and emergency measures – and indirectly – through concern and fear – compelled a high percentage of humanity to self-isolate, stay in their homes or places of residence, avoid contact with other people, and generally limit all social actions and interactions. Or, as discussed earlier, to resist such measures, claiming they are an overreaction or in the name of "freedom." For many people, there is an obvious disconnect between recognizing the fear and concern for the virus and an inability to *see* the actual virus, which lacks the visibility that would make it feel real. Instead, for those who have not experienced or do not accept the severity of the direct effects of the coronavirus, the emergency measures must be accepted on faith, through the mass-communicated rationales that, at times, contrast with what is apparent to our own eyes.

For those who have directly experienced the virus, contracting it themselves or being around someone who has, Covid-19 is painfully visible, even visceral. "My head pounds, a raging ache, so I lie down, just for a nap. I wake hours later, shaking, and finally reach for the thermometer: 99.4. It's low, but undeniable," writes Rachel Ossip in her account of contracting the virus in 2020.[3] Over the span of the pandemic, the people I know who have caught Covid-19 had wildly different experiences – especially after the vaccines were made commonplace and a majority were partially or fully vaccinated. In the first year, a colleague of mine had been infected and recovered; in addition to the usual list of symptoms, they spoke a lot about problems getting tested and other issues related to the ability of the healthcare system to deal with the early stages of the crisis. While Ossip's text includes reflections on specific symptoms and bodily experiences, these accounts are deeply embedded within a psychology of engaging with the contagion – the frustrations of navigating the health system, the *sci-fi* quality of the virus as invader, the manner in which "worrying about the future seems surreal." Her characterization of *living inside the virus*, by which she means "the virus is going on around us and we are also in its haze," is a powerful statement on the futility of all attempts to make sense of the pandemic while inside its effects.[4]

Fang Fang in her *Wuhan Diary* focuses repeatedly on the atmosphere created by the virus, how it affects not just people's

Seeing the Virus

physical but also emotional health. In her 3 February 2020 entry, responding to a documentary in which "the narrator said it was as if someone had 'hit the pause button' on the entire city," Fang Fang writes: "That's right, the entire city is on pause, but for those people whose bodies have already been carted away in bags, it is already over. My heavens! Those undertakers at the crematoriums have never before had to deal with anything like this. But they say it is the doctors who really need our attention, as they are the ones taking care of the living."[5] Here the pause is recognized as a privilege of the living. Writing on 3 April 2020 in Italy, Franco "Bifo" Berardi laments the death of his friend Dr Valter Tarantini, who was listed in *La Repubblica* among "the 68 doctors who died while doing their job in the raging epidemic."[6] In both of these accounts, as well as many others from around the globe, we get a glimpse of a moment of transition when the virus stops being just an idea and becomes bodily, becomes real.

Yet, because this transition brings with it increased concerns and calls for action, many officials and governments actively downplayed the level of the threat even while emphasizing the need to be careful, *un*recognizing the crisis in the process of encouraging recognition. Fang Fang talks about this in the initial refusals to admit the seriousness of the virus when it first emerged, an act that allowed it to spread, including fake reports on its communicability, as well as a reluctance to acknowledge the extent of the pandemic in Wuhan. Throughout (at least) 2020 and 2021, the US increasingly devolved into a series of sometimes discreet and sometimes blatant refusals, which ranged from protests over the enforced emergency measures to calls by the forty-fifth president to stop testing as many people because "by having more tests, we have more cases" – a quote included in the CNN article "Trump Now Says He Wasn't Kidding When He Told Officials to Slow Down Coronavirus Testing, Contradicting Staff" (published June 2020). Such denials conveniently also put high-risk groups, including Black, Latinx, and Indigenous communities, at increased risk. "Policy responses to Covid-19 too often protect the already protected and further expose those who are vulnerable," write Afsoun Afsahi, Emily Beausoleil, Rikki Dean, Selen A. Ercan, and Jean-Paul Gagnon.[7] There is an unfortunate tendency, which seems common during pandemics, to deny the realities of the situation until they can be denied no longer.

Bodies on Bodies

Such is the case with the accumulation of bodies during a plague or pandemic, which make visible the mass death caused by the contagion. In early April 2020, there were rumours that in New York City, due to the overwhelming number of people dying from the virus, the city was going to use public parks for the "temporary interment" of bodies, and bury them in mass trenches. While the "mayor firmly denied there were plans to use a park as a temporary grave site," the outcry from citizens of the city and beyond speaks to an overall concern for the treatment of the dead, even during times of crisis.[8] Imbedded in such a response is a larger question of the relation between a society and its dead. "A horror of the decomposing corpse is

Seeing the Virus

a constant in all civilizations and gave rise to the ritual of mourning performed by the survivors," Michel Ragon writes.[9] Yet, during times of pandemic there is a conflict between belief in mourning the dead and fear of the dead body that may be infected, that may be the bringer of more death.

We can read historical accounts of this conflict in which respecting the dead is put aside because of a strong fear of the diseased corpse. To return to Lucretius's account of the Plague of Athens, several times he notes the tendency for the dead to be left unattended and unburied. At one point, he describes the manner in which "bodies on bodies lay unburied upon the ground in heaps."[10] A similar scene is recounted in Boccaccio's narrative of the Black Death in Florence, which opens and contextualizes his *Decameron*. He writes: "Many there were who passed away in the streets, by day and by night, while scores of those who died indoors only made their neighbours aware of their decease by the stench of their decaying corpse; the whole city was full of those and others dying all over the place."[11] In both accounts, along with numerous others written about plagues and pandemics over the years, there is a strong sense of people being overwhelmed by the fear of infection that causes practices of mourning and, in the worse cases, human decency to be put aside.

In April 2020, images of unclaimed dead being buried in trenches on Hart Island in New York City, with makeshift coffins piled in rows, were repeatedly shared across all media platforms. While there were assurances from public officials that during this "temporary interment," bodies were handled with care and respect, pictures of these mass graves disturbed societal sensibilities and foregrounded ongoing social concern for the dead during Covid-19. Fang Fang also draws attention to this necessary but painful shift, noting that "when the hearse that brings bodies to the crematorium goes from delivering a single body in a coffin to delivering an entire truckload of bodies stuffed into bags" this is a true calamity.[12] Here we witness the necessities of dealing with the dead during a pandemic, when the *horror of the decomposing corpse* is also a (highly) probable vector for the virus to continue spreading. Which poses the impossible question: at what point do we put aside our "humanity" when dealing with the dead and simply protect ourselves?

Accounts of the deaths from Covid-19 in Ecuador were particularly painful to read about. Since the first confirmed cases of the virus in February 2020, the city of Guayaquil, the second largest in Ecuador, was quickly overwhelmed by the sheer number of dead bodies. "Bodies Lie in the Streets of Guayaquil, Ecuador, Emerging Epicenter of the Coronavirus in Latin America" (*Washington Post*, 3 April 2020) and "When Bodies Piled Up: Inside Ecuador's First Coronavirus Hotspot" (*Al Jazeera*, 17 June 2020) are just two of the many newspaper headlines about the situation. As Lise Josefsen Hermann writes: "Hundreds of families were forced to keep their dead relatives' bodies in their homes or on the streets for days until someone from the city could pick them up."[13] The disturbing images from Guayaquil tragically reinforce Lucretius's description of *bodies on bodies*. Patricia Marin Gines admits: "I feel guilty that my father can't have a worthy funeral."[14]

70

Seeing the Virus

My young friend Maya Wilson-Sánchez has family in Ecuador, not in Guayaquil but living in another major city, which has made this whole situation extremely difficult for her. Living in Canada, a country that has "done well" (according to the WHO), she watches this crisis at such a distance that all she can really do is talk with family in Ecuador and hope they stay safe. This is the burden of people living in places in which the virus's effects are less severe than others but who have relatives and friends directly experiencing the brunt of the pandemic; this experience is a type of splitting, or dual vision, having to hold both realities together. Such an existential difficulty exacerbates what has already been a time of personal and social confusion, when formerly unquestionable realities of human life are brought into question. Seeing the virus at this moment becomes, at one and the same time, both recognition and missed recognition of the death that is the contagion.

Masks as Making Visible

For my part, I must acknowledge that I have been lucky and privileged to live in a city (London, Ontario) that has not been affected too badly by Covid-19. The numbers of infected and dead have remained relatively low throughout the pandemic in comparison to nearby cities, such as Toronto. As the title of a June 2021 article makes clear: "Middlesex-London Health Unit Reports 5 New Covid-19 Cases, Zero Deaths" (CTV News). However, the relaxed policies of 2022 have resulted in a significant increase in infections, as a result of which the city, as of 25 July, had "153 deaths attributed to the virus," "two short of the 155 total deaths from Covid-19 in 2021."[15]

It was not until 17 July 2020 that London's top public health official made "face masks mandatory in all indoor public places."[16] At the time, this announcement came as a surprise given the relatively low numbers of people in the city who had contracted the virus, but the reasons given for this decision were concerns about people travelling from cities where the numbers were higher, and as a measure to keep the numbers low while we moved into the next phase, of opening up public spaces. New Democrat MPPs Teresa Armstrong, Peggy Sattler, and Terence Kernaghan also point to the "chaos" of the pandemic situation in the US, which was a cautionary tale for those in neighbouring Canada. But the truth of the matter was, all these conditions had existed for months before the mask mandate was put into place. Why at that moment, when Covid-19 was feeling less emergent than it had in the previous months of the lockdown, was there (finally) a mandate for people to wear masks in public? Certainly not strictly for preventive reasons since, if this were truly the case, these regulations would have been put into place before this moment – for instance, at the same time Toronto instituted its mandate. Given the timing of this preventive measure, I would suggest that this decision was based on an increased need to make people *see* the virus. Having people wearing masks in public spaces is a clear way to make Covid-19 a visible part of daily life.

The visual history of the Spanish flu pandemic similarly reflects this need to make visible what is experientially and liter-

Telephone operators in High River, Alberta, during the Spanish flu pandemic of 1918. From left to right: Gladys Stephenson, Cora Stephenson, Addie McDonald, and Annie Grisdale.

ally, in terms of the actual virus, an invisible threat to the body and to society. And the face mask is the most effective means of making visible, as the innumerable photographs documenting the period demonstrate. Looking at the 1918 photograph of four telephone operators in Alberta – Gladys Stephenson, Cora Stephenson, Addie McDonald, and Annie Grisdale – we understand the context and realities of the influenza outbreak only because they are wearing masks; without the masks, this would simply appear to be an historical photograph of four women.

It is no coincidence that the majority of images from the Spanish flu pandemic picture people with face masks, which in Canada includes a staff photo at the Canadian Bank of Commerce in Calgary and the often-reproduced portrait of three men standing in front of a field. Similarly, in the US, visual documents attest to people going about their daily lives wearing face masks and other (sometimes inventive) protective equipment, as we see in the photographs of a typist in the midst of typing and a letter carrier on his mail route in New York City.

To state the obvious, if these people were not wearing masks, everything would appear normal in the photographs and, aside from the date, we would have no way of knowing a pandemic was occurring.

The mask took on a symbolic quality as "the most distinctive image of the Spanish flu," Catharine Arnold writes. She continues:

> Generally white and fastened behind the head, the mask graduated from medical staff to the civilian population; in many towns and cities it became an offence to go outside without one. Policemen directed traffic in masks, entire family groups were photographed in their masks, including their cats and dogs; a honeymooning couple in San Francisco shyly confessed to their doctor that they wore their masks and nothing else when making love. Surreal and haunting, the photographs of masked figures from this period resemble scenes from a science fiction film.[17]

This characterization of the photographs of people wearing face masks as *surreal* is quite apt and can be applied more broadly to the idea of seeing the virus in everyday life. If we recall the way André Breton defines the "surreal" in the 1924

Seeing the Virus

Letter carrier in New York wearing mask for protection against influenza. New York City, 16 October 1918.

Manifesto of Surrealism, he makes it clear that it is not opposed to the "real" but rather extends the accepted parameters of reality to include elements of life beyond human understanding and reason. During the First World War, an event that overlaps with and overshadowed that of the Spanish flu, Breton served as an intern at the neuropsychiatric centre at Saint-Dizier in Northern France, an experience that profoundly affected his sense of what was real and how we define this concept, *reality*. The wearing of face masks is absolutely sur-real because it shows us part of human reality that is beyond the reality we recognize and accept as *real* – and normal.

So many aspects of these early mask mandates qualify as sur-real, including the initial shortage of masks around the world.

Fang Fang's diary entries throughout January 2020 are filled with references to the shortage of masks in Wuhan, along with mention of the profiteering that was occurring as people desperately tried to get masks. In the US the shortage of personal protective equipment (PPE), including proper masks, led to a shocking suggestion, that front-line healthcare workers should use bandannas. "The U.S. Centers for Disease Control and Prevention has new advice for medical workers desperate for protective gear against Covid-19: Try a bandanna for protection," medical reporter Emily Baumgaertner wrote on 21 March 2020. "The agency, scrambling to advise healthcare workers faced with severe shortages of gear, also recommends that another 'last resort' solution could be a scarf."[18] The lack of PPE was due to the overwhelming and consistent demand throughout the world for protection, especially for healthcare workers dealing directly with the infected, demonstrating a profound lack of preparedness. From the earliest cases of Covid-19 in Canada, the president of the Canadian Federation of Nurses, Linda Silas, voiced concerns about the shortage that did occur. Sadly, two years later in 2022, "she is still desperately calling for more protective equipment for nurses." She is quoted as saying: "The shortage of healthy nurses to address the massive wave of the Omicron variant has meant hospitals and other health institutions have deployed nurses with confirmed cases of Covid-19, and still some are not offered appropriate masks."[19]

A very different form of the surreal can be seen in the development of what had been called the *mask economy*, in which innumerable fashion designers and companies started making

Self-portrait with *Bob's Burgers* mask.

masks of various types, designs, and sensibilities to address a growing desire for new and different mask experiences. This meant the creation of masks that, while serving to help protect their wearer from infection, also functioned on an aesthetic level, as a form of personal expression. The majority of these are novelty designer masks, which include fabric masks such as the Arrow logo mask by Off-White and the Bandana Print Reversible mask by Levi's, as well as promotional masks of which the Dunkin'-ized designed masks by Dunkin' Donuts are a playful example; related to this is the *Bob's Burgers* mask my colleague and friend Maxwell Hyett gave me, for which I repeatedly received compliments.

There has also been a market for "luxury" masks and other forms of PPE, such as Louis Vuitton's "luxury face shield that's designed to be 'both stylish and protective,'" including golden studs engraved with the brand name – a product that, ironically, the CDC does not recommend for proper protection.[20] The title of one article tells us everything we need to know about this trend: "Inside the Surreal 'Mask Economy': Price-Gouging, Bidding Wars, and Armed Guards" (*Fortune* Magazine, April 2020).

Such a desire for "different" masks also became an opportunity to create unique masks. For some, this meant homemade masks that were a form of individual expression, an approach that also functioned against pandemic consumerism. This also led to independent makers creating masks to serve specific needs and desires, in some of the best cases respecting ecological concerns. The example of Rosemarine Textiles, a small Detroit-based sustainable textile studio run by Meghan Navoy, was featured on CNN because of the extreme demand for the masks they were making. "What a weird time to be a business owner!" Navoy writes on her website. "I saw a need for cloth masks and started making them available in early April. I'm plugging away making as many masks as possible to keep up with the demand."[21] While signalling the presence of a contagion, such masks get away from the standard white, medical-looking masks and allow the wearer to experience them more as an accessory and less as *surreal* protection.

Seeing the Virus

Unseeing the Virus

On 11 June 2022, the Province of Ontario (Canada) lifted most of the remaining mask mandates, which had already been loosened but were now, for all intents and purposes, nonexistent except in very select situations. The logic of this transition was interesting, if at times confusing. While governmental mask requirements for hospitals were lifted, many hospitals decided to keep their own masking policies in place, resulting in inconsistencies among the various policies. In Toronto, I was able to use public transit without having to wear a mask but it was still required travelling by train, a policy that remained in place into the fall. When this change was put into practice, I was in Rome (Italy), having arrived just in time for the lifting of their mask mandates on 1 June, after which one could be in most public spaces without a mask – although, again, I was required to wear a mask when I took the train. This transition felt rather abrupt: one day people were wearing masks and the next, surprisingly, a majority were not. In fact, my experience has been that, for many, no longer being required to wear a mask has meant no longer having to *see* Covid-19, meaning that life had finally been truly unpaused.

Following a loosening of regulations in March, the head of Ontario's Covid-19 science advisory table, Dr Peter Jüni, stated: "It's just not pretending it's over, 'There's a light switch and tomorrow we go back to pre-pandemic.' We're not."[22] But this appears to be precisely how people around the world understood this move to take away what were key preventive measures, an indication that the *switch* of the pandemic had been turned off.

79

THE PAUSE

Stated differently, with the dropping of mask mandates and the general move toward returning to "normal" life, humanity appears to believe the pause button had been pushed a second time, allowing life to continue where it was halted by the virus. The public discourse around this assumed end *but not an end* supports the belief that we are in, or are close enough to, a "post-pandemic" moment – that is also an uncanny return to a pre-pandemic state. This reflects a general avoidance of thinking about or dealing with Covid-19 and its effects, a pandemic exhaustion, regardless of the reality of the situation. With many countries loosening restrictions on international travellers, an active attempt to re-attract tourists – especially considering the real concerns regarding the Omicron variant at that time – there was a significant surge in travel around the world. Discussing this trend of "revenge travel," writer Manuela López Restrepo notes that it has been "broadly described as a huge increase in people wanting to make up for time and experiences lost to the pandemic."[23] Such a desire to regain experiences perceived as "missed" is one of many manifestations of the active refusal to continue recognizing the virus, which has been assumed away in an act of existential hubris. Reading declarations of the "end" of the Covid-19 pandemic, I am curious if during the Spanish flu it was also decided, en masse, that it was simply over. Journalist Jon Allsop concludes his survey of the first two years of the "ever-changing pandemic" by noting that, as of early 2022, news consumers seemed less interested in reading about Covid-19: "[A] (frequently high-pitched) debate was playing out in the media as to whether it was time to put the pandemic fully in the past and go back to 'normal.'"[24]

Seeing the Virus

Surreal Visions of the Virus

Judith Butler begins her text "Capitalism Has Its Limits" with the following statement: "The imperative to isolate coincides with a new recognition of our global interdependence during the new time and space of pandemic."[25] Like many theorists responding to Covid-19, Butler focuses on the question of capitalism, specifically considering its limits as defined through the present crisis. Following a similar line of thinking, Bifo writes:

> After forty years of neoliberal acceleration, the race of financial capitalism has suddenly ground to a halt. One, two, three months of global lockdown, a long interruption of the production process and of the global circulation of people and goods, a long period of seclusion, the tragedy of the pandemic … all of this is going to break capitalist dynamics in a way that may be irremediable, irreversible.[26]

At a moment when possibility overwhelmed reality, when the sense of the real failed to live up to the experiences of people facing a truly unknown and strange situation, it is natural to question existing systems such as global capitalism, the limits of which were clearly exposed by the pandemic. This has led, at different points of dealing with Covid-19 and its effects, to a questioning of basic capitalist logics. After first reading about "a Corona Virus that was gaining ground in China" in January 2020, David Harvey tells us that he "immediately thought of the repercussions for the global dynamics of capital accumulation."[27] Attempting to slow the spread of the virus meant putting much of consumer culture on pause, which has been economically devastating.

Given the possibility of an irreversible break in *capitalist dynamics*, again in the process of addressing Covid-19, a number of theorists believe these changes will lead to a type of communism. In *Pandemic! Covid-19 Shakes the World*, Žižek states that the "coronavirus will also compel us to re-invent Communism based on trust in the people and in science."[28] Jean-Luc Nancy goes into rather extreme speculations about a *communovirus* that "essentially puts us on a basis of equality, bringing us together in the need to make a common stand" – immediately before he declares: "In fact, the virus actually does communize us."[29] This is part of a more general utopian reading of the pandemic as a necessary crisis that will force people to come together in addressing such world threats, to recognize the interconnected nature of life and rethink human existence accordingly. Yet these optimisms that were an important part of the early critical thinking around the pandemic began to feel misplaced or even naive when we reached 2022. Even the well-rehearsed claims that, given the global nature of the crisis, "we are all in this together" appeared to be a mere slogan were depressingly distant from the realities of the social, political, and economic disparities around the globe that the virus has highlighted.

While I do enjoy the (verbose) claims that the Covid-19 pandemic might have been the end of capitalism, it is important to recognize the complexities of this relationship. Given the lengthy history of capitalism, which demonstrates just how

Seeing the Virus

adaptable it can be, its rather amazing resilience and ability to continue its logics beyond what would logically seem possible, the likelihood that it can weather this crisis is high. In fact, starting in the latter half of 2022, we witnessed the return of capitalist logics with a vengeance through a global push toward getting life back to "normal" – which seems to be code for a return to experiences facilitated in and through consumer capitalism. Instead of an "end" of capitalism, it may be more helpful to consider the pause as a temporary ideological closure, reflecting the ways many businesses had to literally shut down during the major lockdowns, especially in 2020. This raises an important question: what would this pausing of capitalism look like?

One of the more disquieting experiences I have had during the pandemic was the sight of empty parking lots during the first lockdown – reminiscent, as a colleague pointed out, of the images in Ed Ruscha's 1967 artist's bookwork *Thirty-Four Parking Lots in Los Angeles*. I am referring to the mega-parking lots located in front of large chain stores, theatres, amusement parks of various kinds, casinos, and, especially, shopping malls. When I was young, the parking lots of malls were only full on weekends or on peak holidays, but for at least the last decade or so they have tended to be near capacity most days; seeing these lots empty is a sure sign something is wrong. One only has to think about the many science fiction or disaster films that use desolate, emptied urban environments to communicate devastation and, in most cases, a serious threat to human existence. Common themes include: (1) environmental threats, such as the 2019 film *IO*, in which the air has become toxic to humans; (2) biochemical threats, such as the 2007 film *I Am Legend*, in which a virus has rendered the Earth uninhabitable; (3) alien threats, such as the 2010 film *Skyline*, in which alien invaders capture and consume human beings. Witnessing a nearby parking lot with no cars was reminiscent of many haunting scenes in films and television programs of this type. A big regret I have is not taking photographs of these empty parking lots, which remain one of the most important visual experiences I had during the pandemic.

In summer 2020, as businesses started to reopen in Canada following the first major lockdown, a change that reflected similar openings around the world, the strangeness was still present – and has arguably remained a consistent part of the pause. One headline regarding the reopenings, specifically referencing Montreal, read: "The First Day of Downtown Shopping during Covid-19: A Little Surreal" (CTV News, May 2020). The simplicity of this return has become increasingly complicated as the pandemic has continued, with shoppers and businesses having to adjust to new realities of social life. Going to the supermarket, I had to wear a mask and keep my distance from other people, which included respecting the two metres of social distancing, visually demarcated on the floor with stickers of abstract feet, as well as the installation of large Plexiglas barriers separating me from the cashiers; when these requirements were removed in 2022 and the experience was "normal" again, signs of this hyperconscious mode of engagement remained, even without, for the majority of people, the corresponding action. Will *normal* ever be normal as long as the possibilities of the virus continue? Have we truly *un-paused*

Seeing the Virus

while Covid-19 continues to infect people around the globe? Part of this reality is the undefined, maybe even un-definable, act of envisioning life in a pandemic. Scenes of empty parking lots, of lines of people wearing masks, of mass concern over supposed shortages of toilet paper – it really *is* surreal.

A Theory of
Social Distancing

tens, hundreds of simultaneous actions, micro events,
each one of which necessitates postures, movements,
specific expenditures of energy
– Georges Perec[1]

At a Distance

Isolation, the result of the demands of social distancing, is as unexpected today and as complete as can be. In this moment, during the extended period of the Covid-19 crisis, we live under different rules and in spite of everything, somewhere at the margins of history, we await – a refracted sense of self, one in which the events being discussed and documented around the world and the realities of our own personal experiences appear incompatible. This is the dilemma of the pause.

A profound and disturbing existential distance haunts humanity during times of pandemic. Not just now within our present outbreak, but more broadly in accounts of past contagions that have undermined our *common* – Hannah Arendt would say *communal* – *sense* relations between our lives and the world around us. Michel Foucault defines the form of the plague as "at once real and imaginary," a contradictory state

A Theory of Social Distancing

that plays on the misperceptions of people who attempt to fix experiences of it into an existing sense of "order."[2] At times imperceptible, the difference of life under the shadow of pandemic undermines even the most basic assumptions about the realities of our experiences. Referring to the psychoanalyst Gabriel Tupinambá, Slavoj Žižek describes this condition in the following manner: "[I]f there is no great change in our daily reality, then the threat is experienced as a spectral fantasy nowhere to be seen and all the more powerful for that reason."[3] In this state, we are left with little sense of the real and limited ability to imagine beyond these failed realities.

As Albert Camus writes in *The Plague*: "In appearance nothing has changed."[4] Which makes it difficult for many to understand why social distancing practices or mask mandates were put in place.

For those people in critical medical situations, in which Covid is an obvious and lethal threat, the societal insistence on social distancing and self-isolation, as well as the various enforcements of these and other measures, is for the most part understood as acceptable. During the first months of the pandemic in Italy, a number of the people I know who live in Rome repeatedly expressed outrage in their social media posts against those "selfish" people not respecting the quarantine. In the fall of 2021, as most of the professors I know were continuing to struggle with the limits of online teaching, a friend and colleague who was still recovering from contracting the virus was continually baffled by the demands that the university consider some in-person classes; now that we have returned to (mostly) in-person teaching as of fall 2022, many questions remain in terms of protecting staff, faculty, and students as opposed to accommodating the desire for being IRL (in real life).

Against the appearance that *nothing has changed*, many do not have the luxury of ignoring the various realities of the pandemic. Those with compromised immune systems, those who suffer from long Covid, as well as those who seem especially susceptible to the virus need to remain vigilant even within environments where most people are more than happy to forget the pandemic even occurred. It is through this problematic of perception, the need or lack of preventive measures, that I would like to explore the concept of *social distancing*.

What Is Social Distancing?

Social distancing is one of a number of commonly used non-pharmaceutical interventions (NPIs) that help limit the spread of disease. As opposed to taking a vaccine and other medicine, NPIs can be employed by individuals and are therefore critical to any society's attempts to resist infectious outbreaks; one does not need any outside tools to physically separate oneself from other people. The CDC on their website in October 2020 defined "social distancing" as "keeping a safe space between yourself and other people who are not from your household." The actual practice of social or physical distancing is described in the following manner: "[S]tay at least 6 feet (about 2 arms' length) from other people who are not from your household in both indoor and outdoor spaces."[5] It should be noted that

A Theory of Social Distancing

Social distancing sign, Toronto 2022.

this differs from the CDC definition found on its webpage in April 2020, which, in addition to the six feet rule, also included two points now absent: "Do not gather in groups" and "Stay out of crowded places and avoid mass gatherings." The elimination of these public restrictions is telling, especially given the political and economic pressures forced onto the CDC by the American government.

While the CDC functioned as one of the main sources for defining and understanding such practices, there are innumerable other places to get information on social distancing practices from various perspectives. We can look, for example, at the "Report of the WHO-China Joint Mission on Coronavirus Disease 2019 (Covid-19)," which describes early social distancing practices in China:

> At the national level, the State Council extended the Spring Festival holiday in 2020, all parts of the country

THE PAUSE

actively cancelled or suspended activities like sport events, cinema, theatre, and schools and colleges in all parts of the country postponed reopening after the holiday. Enterprises and institutions have staggered their return to work. Transportation Departments setup thousands of health and quarantine stations in national service areas, and in entrances and exits for passengers at stations. Hubei Province adopted the most stringent traffic control measures, such as suspension of urban public transport, including subway, ferry and long-distance passenger transport. Every citizen has to wear a mask in public. Home support mechanisms were established. As a consequence of all of these measures, public life is very reduced.[6]

In response to the question "What can other countries learn from the way China has approached Covid-19?" the head of the Chinese Center for Disease Control and Prevention, George Gao, stated:

> Social distancing is the essential strategy for the control of any infectious diseases, especially if they are respiratory infections. First, we used "nonpharmaceutical strategies," because you don't have any specific inhibitors or drugs and you don't have any vaccines. Second, you have to make sure you isolate any cases. Third, close contacts should be in quarantine: We spend a lot of time trying to find all these close contacts, and to make sure they are quarantined and isolated. Fourth,

A Theory of Social Distancing

suspend public gatherings. Fifth, restrict movement, which is why you have a lockdown, the *cordon sanitaire* in French.[7]

Since the effects of the virus were first experienced in China, this becomes an important perspective for considering the ways social distancing was enacted following the March 2020 declaration of the novel coronavirus as a pandemic worldwide.

In her article in Johns Hopkins University's publication *Hub*, senior writer Katie Pearce provides a more colloquial description. She writes: "Social distancing is a public health practice that aims to prevent sick people from coming in close contact with healthy people in order to reduce opportunities for disease transmission. It can include large-scale measures like canceling group events or closing public spaces, as well as individual decisions such as avoiding crowds."[8] One movement with the self-declared aim of stopping the pandemic, defined in part through a Self-Quarantine Manifesto that lists twelve actions for making a difference, gives us a blatant mandate: "Stay The Fuck Home!"[9] In such everyday appeals, we can recognize the practical nature of this mode of prevention, the goal of which is to have people distance themselves from various social interactions, on both larger scales (bars, arenas, theatres, schools, museums, and the like) and smaller scales (meetings, personal visits, and the like), with the aim of limiting the spread of the virus. To state the obvious: if Covid-19 primarily infects through a form of close contact with people who are infected, the simplest way to limit infections is to limit possible moments of contact.

Levels of Compliance

With social distancing practices in place throughout much of the world, there was little doubt about the effectiveness of these measures that, where applied thoroughly, have helped to at least slow the progress of the virus. In countries where citizens are more resistant to or less accepting of such measures, including the wearing of masks, the number of infections and deaths is notably (if not exceedingly) higher than in countries where compliance is more widespread. Living in Canada, it is all but impossible to see the infection rates in the US as anything but surreal – with the virus causing, as of 9 October 2020, a reported 213,000 American deaths in comparison to a reported 9,586 Canadian deaths. "The United States could have been in a similar situation as Canada," Zack Beauchamp wrote in May 2020. "We have the world's largest economy and its finest academic institutions; the Canadians show us that, had our political leadership marshaled these resources in the right ways and at the right times, some significant numbers of American lives would likely have been saved."[10] The question of compliance certainly is a key issue, given that most Canadians throughout the pandemic were generally accepting of the preventive measures – with the notable exception of the 2022 truckers' protest – as opposed to a great number of Americans who openly flaunt their non-compliance as an expression of "freedom."

The question of following social distancing practices has, as many predicted at the outset of the pandemic, become quite fraught. This has been particularly true within the US

A Theory of Social Distancing

where necessary limits imposed to ensure people's safety are defined as undermining the (neoliberal) powers of personal freedom. We can divide people into three general categories of levels of compliance.

In the first are people who treat social distancing as doctrine or personal law. They are not simply following the guidelines but are taking the measures as almost ends in themselves. These are the people who do not simply stay the requisite 6 feet away from you on the street but maintain maximum distance from any and all other people in public spaces. In extreme cases, people in this category are the ones who quite literally hurry away when they see you even at a distance, who dramatically leap aside if they imagine you are too close, expressing a panicked agitation or even anger at anyone who is perceived as violating *their* space. Here there is an overarching sense of fear that defines a person's response, which in the worse cases lends itself to moralizing on other people's adherence to these "rules."

The second category includes the majority of people. They follow the general practices of their communities and overall are cognizant of both the personal and social concerns that necessitate these measures, so maintain a realistic sense of why these actions are in place. This includes a basic understanding of the relative nature of practices such as social distancing, which requires one to critically think about what is appropriate and needed in a given situation – rather than blanket treatments of all actions and all situations. Fear is not the driving force of this compliance; rather, social distancing is followed out of a larger sense of personal and civic precaution.

In "Distance Must Be Maintained," Aaron Timms outlines the shift toward conscious movement through the space of New York City during the pandemic. He writes:

> Some are good at playing the six-foot separation game. Others range across the sidewalk with lazy disregard for the new conventions, two abreast, arms pumping, social-spatial awareness set to zero. I magnetize myself to walls or duck into the oncoming traffic whenever someone approaches in the opposite direction, pause to let older pedestrians pass whenever a sub-six foot collision course is looming, speed up, slow down, cross if things look emptier on the other side. Stripped of its innocence, the dart-and-weave common to the New York driver or the Manhattan pedestrian has been exported to every walking corner of the city.[11]

This description aims to communicate how Timms personally navigates the new realities of urban travel, accepting the necessary limits of interpersonal contact due to the threats of infection. Timms demonstrates a level of personal responsibility that locates him within the second category, focusing here on communicating his awareness of the threats given the dense context of the city and, in April 2020 when this text was written, the seriousness of the situation in New York City.

The third category of people are those whose awareness of or concerns for the necessity of the preventive measures is, to borrow Timms's phrasing, *set to zero*. These individuals do not follow the basic parameters of social distancing, either out of a

A Theory of Social Distancing

lack of appreciation for the measures or in active defiance of them. Innumerable stories have filled the news, especially coming out of the US, of people who flaunt their non-distancing efforts. One disturbing example of this was the so-called Covid parties, organized by young Americans, mostly in the first year of the pandemic, which reporters Faith Karimi and Jamiel Lynch describe as "a disturbing competition where people who have coronavirus attend and the first person to get infected receives a payout."[12] Implicit in this "game" is the assumption that the virus was not a real threat; "I think I made a mistake," a thirty-year-old man is said to have admitted on his deathbed to Dr Jane Appleby, chief medical officer at Methodist Hospital in San Antonio. "I thought this was a hoax, but it's not."[13] In this case, there appears to be a belief that the pandemic is an elaborate conspiracy, which has encouraged many to dismiss the necessity of social distancing and other preventive measures. While for others, it must be said, the refusal is simply an act of selfishness.

Agamben is a noteworthy case study for this latter category, given his resistance to the emergency measures, which he outright claims are "frantic, irrational, and absolutely unwarranted."[14] "Other human beings," Agamben writes in a follow-up text, "are now seen only as potential contaminators to be avoided at all costs or at least to keep at a distance of at least one metre."[15] Throughout his writings on the pandemic, there is a sense of concern for the ways the body was being treated in the basest of ways – as *bare life*, to use his term – a sacrifice Agamben argues is more harmful than helpful. In a short text on "Social Distancing," written in April 2020, he states: "What social distancing measures and panic have created is surely a mass, but a mass that is, so to speak, inverted and composed of individuals who are keeping themselves at any cost at a distance – a non-dense, rarefied mass."[16] Read from this perspective, his concerns become more clearly directed not at the need for or lack of the specific measure – although his non-compliance is blatant – but rather with our blind (ethical and political) acceptance of these practices aimed at disallowing human contact and freedoms in the name of this current health crisis.

The quintessential quality of this third category is an extreme sense of individual rights and freedoms, which are privileged over all larger social and cultural concerns – even, one might say, over the right to life itself. Compliance is therefore understood as diametrically opposed to individual "freedom," which conveniently supports resisting any limits not desired by the given individual. Such an attitude of exceptionalism allows individuals to see themselves as the exception to a given rule – a way of understanding fostered by neoliberal capitalism, which incites us to consume without regard for personal, political, environmental, or social consequences. As Benjamin Bratton makes clear: "Freedom means freedom from supervision, and so the heroic individual resists the oppressive and pervasive societal manipulation, finally realizing his solitary existential triumph."[17] This is precisely what makes this third category of compliance potentially dangerous, the way it feeds into fantasies of the hero who stands alone against society yet is somehow fighting for society's interests; but the pandemic is not a superhero movie; it is a global threat to the human species that must be taken seriously.

A Theory of Social Distancing

Social Media in the Pandemic

The fact that the pandemic is taking place in an age of social media is highly significant, not just because of the way information is shared and experienced, but also for how this information is shaped by the medium itself. At the outset of the crisis, a number of governmental and private authorities turned to key social media platforms as a means of communicating vital information quickly and efficiently. It also became a tool for individuals to share their own experiences with Covid-19 and its effects, providing more personal accounts that speak to everyday realities otherwise passed over – Fang Fang's early posts on the Chinese platform Sina Weibo are an ideal example. Yet these same platforms also spread all manner of misinformation and disinformation, which many have argued are "as much a threat to global public health as the virus itself."[18] This dual character of social media is the result of privileging communications to as many people as possible (the most *clicks*), often understood as democratically open (free) to all voices, a result of which is diminished focus on the quality of the information communicated.

It is worth defining this term that has now become so ubiquitous. After presenting a series of existing definitions, Caleb Carr and Rebecca Hayes provide their own: "Social media are Internet-based channels that allow users to opportunistically interact and selectively self-present, either in real-time or asynchronously, with both broad and narrow audiences who derive value from user-generated content and the perception of interaction with others."[19] I want to highlight two elements in this definition that are important for our discussion. The first is the idea that these platforms allow users to interact *opportunistically* and present themselves *selectively*, an approach that places emphasis not on thorough engagements with topics but rather on partial treatments of various subjects. The second is the specific phrase that ends the definition, which explicitly points at the way *interaction with others* is understood as personal *perceptions* without a need for external support. To state the obvious, social media privileges individual perceptions and responses over rigorous or critical discussions of a topic.

On the one hand, many platforms have shown themselves to be dynamic modes of sharing and even generating different kinds of information, quickly and with a premium on user-generated valuations. This is the power of social media, which pushes existing limits of public discourse – examples include the Occupy Movement, the Arab Spring, the Me Too movement, and Black Lives Matter. On the other hand, there are continuing problems with the foregrounding of opinions and *opportunistic* information, which are too often treated as "truths." Such an uncritical approach, in which claims are merely accepted without proper support or understanding, has led to the common acceptance of what otherwise, with even a little bit of thought and investigation, would be recognized as ludicrous ideas and theories. This aspect of social media has become all the more concerning when its platforms became the main source for communicating information about the pandemic to various publics.

An obvious example of this is the (unfortunately) lingering concerns that the Covid-19 vaccines contain microchips. The

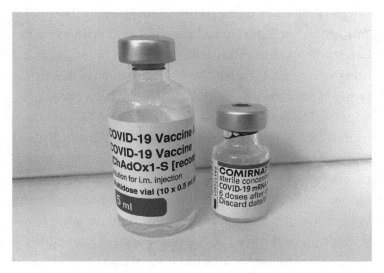

Covid-19 vaccine bottles.

Mayo Clinic's Facebook page presented a "myth buster" post on this topic:

> MYTH: Covid-19 vaccines were developed to control the population through "microchip" tracking or "nano-transducers" in the human brain.
>
> FACT: There is no vaccine "microchip," and the vaccine will not track people or gather personal information into a database.[20]

Repeated attempts have been made to dispel this belief, yet, as the headline of one article stated in July 2021, "20% of Americans Believe Government Is Injecting Microchips in

Covid-19 Vaccines, Survey Finds." Based on an *Economist/YouGov* poll, this "debunked theory" continued to find followers who used this (mis)information as a rationale for not being vaccinated. President Joe Biden is quoted in this article, saying of social media companies, "They're killing people." In response, Facebook spokesman Kevin McAlister said in a statement: "We will not be distracted by accusations which aren't supported by the *facts*. The *fact* is that more than 2 billion people have viewed *authoritative* information about Covid-19 and vaccines on Facebook, which is more than any other place on the internet" (emphasis added).[21] Aside from the humorously strategic use of the word "facts," this statement plays upon the idea that the quantity of information is of highest value – *more than 2 billion people have viewed* – a status that makes it "authoritative." But no number of *views* makes the microchip theory true, no matter how *authoritative* one's experience may be of this (dis)information.

Part of the problem is the medium itself. We often forget that it operates as a nexus of mass user-found and user-generated information, purposefully developed with few to no mechanisms in place to evaluate that information beyond the opinions of the users themselves. While this is consistently perceived as democratic, what results is a severely limited spectrum of possibilities that all support the perspectives of those engaging with the platform – creating echo chambers. In her article "Social Media Use during Social Distancing," Brenda K. Wiederhold writes: "What we see on social media is shaped by algorithms that typically highlight the content that will draw the most attention, not necessarily the content that is verified as correct. This attention to popularity over accuracy may be partially responsible for the spread of misinformation online."[22] Soon after this, Wiederhold refers to "infodemic," the term created by the WHO, "an overabundance of information – some accurate and some not – that makes it hard for people to find trustworthy sources and reliable guidance when they need it."[23] Drawing on the famous phrase by Marshall McLuhan, we might say that the medium of social media is an unquestioning message.

Even with accurate information, the emphasis on an openness of interpretation that pervades social media allows for and even encourages distortions and misunderstandings. Here, reflective of the third level of compliance discussed above, the notion of absolute "freedom" prevails over all other concerns: freedom from supervision, freedom of information, freedom to say whatever one wants. Paired with our society of celebrity, we see public figures such as Elon Musk making claims based on superficial interpretations of posted information about the virus, such as his 19 March 2020 tweet, "Kids are essentially immune" – a statement immediately refuted by innumerable medical authorities. "Have you seen the TikTok where someone turns into a zombie after getting a Covid-19 vaccine?" asks CBC Kids News contributor Isabelle MacNeil, "That's pretty funny – and obviously fake. But other videos can be pretty convincing, even though they aren't actually real."[24] It is pretty funny that a Grade 10 student demonstrates a greater ability to critically interpret information on the pandemic than many celebrity "authorities" on social media.

Social Media / Social Distancing

While the prominence of social media was well established before the pandemic, the increased dependence on virtual interactions and communications, a direct result of the measures put in place to slow the spread of the virus, challenged people's abilities to be social in meaningful ways. This shift from in-person to virtual experience transferred much of people's social lives into the digital realm, a transition (translation) that has foregrounded key problems with this mode of relationality. In the early days of the pandemic, many commentators claimed that the younger generations who grew up on social media would have an easier time adjusting to the situation, a belief that ended up not being true. Ultimately, the shift in experiencing the social at a distance and the corresponding pause in physical interactions proved to invite a larger societal question about the limitations of human socialization in the contemporary world.

For the twentieth-century political philosopher Hannah Arendt, the modern understanding of the social constitutes a realm that "is neither public nor private, strictly speaking."[25] The traditional separation between a public life that exists in the world and a private life of the home is complicated through the concept of the social realm, which, in line with technological and cultural developments in Europe throughout the nineteenth century, allows public and private to exist together. Arendt uses the example of domestic items sold in public for use in private – such as soap. For generations, soap was made in the home for the home, but with the expansion of capitalism

A Theory of Social Distancing

it became a mass-produced item available in stores. The care of the self becomes a hybrid issue for modern individuals, who increasingly address private concerns through public items and discourses.

The same general way of thinking can be applied to social media, which blurs the distinction between notions of public and private experience. On the one hand, social media platforms such as Facebook, Twitter (changed to X in April 2023), Instagram, and others depend upon people taking private aspects of their lives and making them public. "As the recent pandemic (2020–21) further highlighted, the use [of] the social media is not only an important means by which individuals share their lives with others, but can often be the only means by which to do so."[26] In a study on the way teenagers negotiate context in social media, a seventeen-year-old Chinese American named Meixing is quoted as saying: "I mean I do care about privacy, but if I found someone that I could trust then my first instinct would be to share stuff with that person."[27] On the other hand, this active facilitation of sharing private information in public has defined a new sense of self, one in which individual experience, to be truly meaningful, must be recognized publicly through "sharing" within the experience economy. It is not enough to merely post information; one is expected to *advertise* oneself through the specific forms of shared experiences one posts, turning select aspects of life into a public display – which, in the case of big data, has become a vital source of marketable information.

The *social* of social distancing shares in this dynamic. Through its practice of creating spatial pauses between bodies, it signals a mode of personal separation that must (strictly speaking) be understood as neither public nor private. The notion of the social functions as a way of thinking about individual experience as essentially relational, a perspective that is directly called into question with a mandate to limit physical interactions with other bodies in space – which, somewhat ironically, is precisely how those relations are experienced within social media. In fact, inherent in this modern conception of the social is the question of distance, inferred in social media and literalized in social distancing. Within the pause, there is this necessity that an individual exist apart from direct experience, putting pressure on this particular quality of the social in modern and contemporary cultures.

Yet, the difference between these two enactments of the social is extremely telling. With social media, as well as digital communications technologies in general, the distance between individuals communicating with each other is something that is celebratorily overcome – even understood as neutralized – enabling relationships that are not dependent on physical proximity. This quality made such ways of experiencing the world particularly vital during the pandemic. As Tong King Lee and Dingkun Wang say in their introduction to the collection *Translation and Social Media Communication in the Age of the Pandemic*:

> The virtual and ever-proliferating networks of social media represent the obverse of our physical world in these pandemic times, as characterized by impeded

A Theory of Social Distancing

travel and restricted mobilities. Prolonged isolation at homes or in hotels and altered proxemics arising from distancing measures have intensified feelings of estrangement. This has prompted individuals to volume up on social media communications, as if in compensation for their loss in pre-Covid interactivities.[28]

With social distancing, the role of distance is protective and therefore grounded in the wellness of the social body. Yet, while individuals keeping a safe distance from people serves the larger health needs of the society, this *prolonged isolation* does challenge individual needs for social interactions and contact. The social is a paradox (*para-doxa*) in social distancing, designating a dual state of safeguarding the health of society and safeguarding the health of individuals in society, prerogatives that at times are in direct conflict.

Measures of a Pandemic

Walking home from the supermarket during a lockdown in 2020, I passed two women on opposite sides of a small street having a conversation. As I approached and they said their goodbyes, the woman on the side of the street that I inhabited turned to me and said, "Sorry for shouting." To which I responded, "No worries, it is just part of our day." After this encounter, I stopped on the sidewalk and wrote about this exchange, which felt like an important occurrence to me at the time. While maintaining a safe distance, these two neighbours continued to be present in each other's lives. In particular, the idea of witnessing measurement caught my attention.

Social distancing has had a number of effects on the ways people live their lives, some more obvious than others. There is the physical distance that it mandates, which around the world is commonly two metres – "while in China, it is said to be one and a half metres."[29] At times, this is easy to follow, such as the case of the two women mentioned above or when standing in line; at other times, it can be a challenge, such as walking in a supermarket where a number of factors (width of the lanes, looking for specific items, number of people) can cause individuals to forget about the distance between themselves and others. Less obvious, perhaps, are the mental or psychological effects of negotiating this proscribed social distance, which requires that one be conscious of ways of moving through the world that one typically does not think about. As social anthropologist Xiang Biao states: "The 2-metre distance does not necessarily change our interpersonal relationships; but it can provide a perspective that enables us to experience or rethink the subtle grammars in interpersonal relationships. These grammars were previously hidden, but now they suddenly have appeared."[30] A key effect of social distancing is the way it has exposed, as with most *grammars*, the (living) inconsistencies within the given grammars of "distancing" oneself.

By looking at the major inconsistencies, it is possible to define different moments of the pandemic, specifically in relation to the question of the pause. Near the outset, in 2020, it con-

A Theory of Social Distancing

tributed to the empty streets and extremely limited number of cars visible in cities, as well as closed businesses and the emergence of wildlife in (human) social spaces; it very much felt as if life had been paused. During the "second wave," throughout parts of 2021, it became more about negotiating spaces and attempting to continue limiting the spread of the virus while also reclaiming parts of life, bit by bit; the pause was arousing more anxiety and resistance. Throughout the latter part of 2021 and into 2022, we have seen a move from general concerns with the numbers of infected to an outright resistance to not living a "normal" life; as of June 2022, the mask mandates had mostly been lifted and social distancing had been reduced to a light suggestion as we witnessed attempts to *unpause*, to the point where in 2023 most of these experiences feel very much in the past. While Agamben believed this *singularly formulated* practice of "*social* distancing" would remain after other measures ended, becoming "a new paradigm of societal organization," it appears to have instead become similar to background noise that some notice but most ignore.[31] Although the reasons for the measure remained relevant, with Covid and its variants continuing to take lives around the world, most people have lost the incentive to remain conscious of this part of their lives.

A theory of social distancing must be grounded not in the result, of being two metres away from other people, but in the act of materially and psychologically navigating an appropriately *social* distance, successful or not. It confronts the questions of (conscious) measure, the ways individual and social bodies negotiate the realities of mass contagion. I am speaking

THE PAUSE

here of times when parts or all of humanity are under mortal threat, plagues of various sorts that have tested and helped define the human throughout recorded histories. Nothing makes us aware of our own limits as a species quite like a threat to life itself, especially when we get a glimpse of this threat on a larger scale – I believe an (under)estimated 6.31 million deaths worldwide as of June 2022 has given us just such a glimpse. Through social distancing, we become hyperconscious of how we exist in the world, our relation to the spaces we occupy and the other bodies within them, as well as with the limits of our own control over our existence. This is a vital quality of the pause, understood not just in relation to the current pandemic but also as a repeated temporary delay or hesitation or refrain within the process of a lived history.

Asynchronicity

Pause.
– Georges Perec[1]

Reading Books in the Pause

During one of the many weeks or months in which I was in lockdown, toward the end of another vague, timeless evening I had learned so well how to spend, I happened to be browsing for books on the websites of a number of presses. This was a good way of occupying myself and doing research of a sort, especially in keeping up to date on the books being published on the topic of Covid-19. Another reason was the sales that many of these presses offered during that stage in the pandemic, which in part aimed to help them through a difficult time financially but also supported the important act of *reading in a time of self-isolation* – as it read on the Verso website in March 2020. As many people found themselves isolated, not just from the outside world but, as the pandemic wore on, also from a larger sense of their familiar reality, the act of reading became an important strategy for negotiating this pause. While in lockdown or at moments of isolation, reading provided an alternative reality to the, at times, unbearable one we found ourselves within. Yet even when the restrictions were mostly lifted and people's lives had mostly returned to "normal," the practice of reading remained integral to engaging with and understanding the pause in its complexity.

A key reason for this, I would suggest, is the book itself, which acts as a self-contained world that one can imaginatively inhabit – at a time when the "real" world felt uninhabitable. At its most basic, a book consists of a sequence of pages (leaves) that are bound together into the material form of the *codex*, which presents information that begins at one point and ends at another. After the invention of the printing press, books were standardized to such a degree that readers in different locations in the world could refer to statements on specific pages, allowing for shared asynchronous readings of the same words and sentences. Anyone, for example, who reads the 2022 publication of Albert Camus's *The Plague* by Vintage Books, as translated by Laura Marris, will be able to turn to page 7 and see the following sentences: "But perhaps it's time to drop the commentary and precautions of language and get down to the narrative itself. Explaining the first days requires a few details."[2] This quality of experiencing information apart from the place or time of the person or people who wrote it, while part of any act of reading, including eBooks and other digital formats, is specifically employed in the modern book form as a means of describing and creating realities, both fictional and real.

It is worth recalling Catherine Malabou's idea of *quarantine within the quarantine*, which I previously tied to the idea of

Asynchronicity

writing but here want to think about in relation to modern traditions of reading. During the eighteenth century, "reading takes on its recognizably modern contours" as it "begins its long shift to a private, leisure activity," which Annika Mann, in her book *Reading Contagion*, describes as a transformation from "the distant contact provided by print into an immediate affective experience, one often described via the language of contagion."[3] In a very real sense, the act of reading a book defines a specifically modern form of experience that is at one and the same time cultural and personal, imagined and real. One reads a book alone – as if *quarantined* – even when with other people, yet the book is also an experience that one shares asynchronously with a multitude of individuals, often in vastly different places and times than oneself. Reading is an act that embraces the physical and psychological individuation that is foregrounded in self-isolation, social distancing, and other modes of separation vital to protecting self and society in times of contagion.

In this way, the book defines an asynchronous mode of individual experience that is uniquely qualified to address the spatial and temporal realities of living in a pandemic. Reading is an act of being present, engaging with words and ideas as one encounters them, yet distanced from the world at the same time, as one inhabits the world of the text. This disconnect has parallels to life within the pause, in which presence and absence fluctuate as the narrative of the contagion develops and changes – so-called waves function like chapters. Why not turn to these self-contained worlds of books when you yourself are in the process of physical (self-isolation) or psychological (the pause) self-containment? Reading in a time of contagion makes more apparent the asynchronicity of presence that quintessentially grounds experience within a crisis of human imagination.

What are You Reading?

An article posted on the Medicine Hat Public Library blog in March 2020 lists four ways that reading can "save your sanity during Covid-19": (1) reading for stress relief, (2) reading as an escape, (3) reading helps you sleep better, and (4) reading makes you more compassionate to others and yourself.[4] Among the strategies for dealing with the pause of the pandemic, reading in its various guises – as fun, entertainment, information, education, research, and so on – imaginatively connects inner and outer worlds through a collective of individual readers. At a moment when our sense of space and time is distorted, the inner world of a book feels stable and gives us a sense of control. Marcello Giovanelli, a researcher on the Lockdown Library Project, noted the way a lot of people who responded to the survey on reading habits during the first lockdown in the UK "spoke of books as old friends," describing reading as therapeutic, a space where they could safely escape.[5] It is therefore quite fascinating to consider the question of what people are reading while within the pandemic.

On a general level, we know that a surprising number of people have been reading historical books specifically on plagues and pandemics. Two that stand out are Boccaccio's *De-*

Asynchronicity

cameron and Camus's *The Plague*. "During the Covid-19 pandemic, it is particularly rewarding to (re)read the *Decameron*," writes Katrin Rupp, "since our current experience of a global viral disease likely comes to bear on how we react to the plight of the plague that Boccaccio describes."[6] It is not only the resonance of the subject matter, the fact of reading about a pandemic while in a pandemic, but also the experiential parallels that allow readers to see the narrative in new ways. This is also the case with Elisabeth Stelson's reading of Camus in late March 2020. As she notes: "I lay propped up by a mound of pillows in bed, alternating between reading Albert Camus's *The Plague* (*La Peste*) and closing my eyes, too tired and too pained for much else."[7] Her analysis of the book, which she acknowledges she has read previously, foregrounds the necessary change in interpreting *The Plague* once the suffering described by Camus can be imagined by the reader in more of a *right way*.

We also know about specific choices of readings through both conversations with people and writings in which the author tells us what they are reading. Beyond mere interest, the knowledge of such reading habits points toward the types of inner worlds that people gravitated toward. While talking with my friend Janice Gurney in fall 2020, she mentioned three books that she was working through: Hartley Coleridge's 1851 *Poems* (published in two volumes), *The Roman Poets*, edited by Peter Washington, and *The Echoing Green: Poems of Fields, Meadows, and Grasses*, edited by Cecily Parks. In the second part of his "Diary of the Psycho-Deflation," Bifo tells us about books he has read or is in the process of reading, including Sara Mesa's *Cara de pan*, Cristina Morales's *Lectura facil*, and Italo

113

Calvino's *Orlando furioso di Ludovico Ariosto raccontato da Italo Calvino*, as well as the Azerbaijani writer Babine (Banine).[8] And in the small reading group I was part of in the first summer of the pandemic that included my friends Dot Tuer, Alberto Gomez, and Emily Dickson, we read several of Bifo's books. We may recall that Catherine Malabou was rereading *Confessions* by Jean-Jacques Rousseau. The Bengali-American author Jhumpa Lahiri discusses her rereading of Antonio Gramsci's *Letters from Prison*, noting: "while I first discovered Gramsci's letters when I was moving from one place to another, my second discovery, sitting in the Firestone Library at Princeton during Covid-19, occurred in an historic moment characterized by stillness."[9]

My own reading included three obsessions, which loosely cover the pandemic years of 2020 to 2022. In the beginning, I found myself reading books by Georges Perec, starting with *The Art of Asking Your Boss for a Raise* and *An Attempt at Exhausting a Place in Paris*, followed by various readings related to Oulipo – Ouvroir de Littérature Potentielle (Workshop for Potential Literature) – of which Perec was a member. This focus took a back seat in the latter part of 2021 when my focus shifted to Albert Camus, particularly *The Plague*, which I finished reading in fall 2022 just as I had nearly completed the first draft of the manuscript for this current book. While many elements of this novel resonate with the current moment, one in particular haunts me, Camus's description of what enables the narrator of the story to "take on the historian's task." He writes:

114

Asynchronicity

"The narrator of this story therefore has his own: first of all what he witnessed, then what others witnessed, since, through his role, he ended up collecting the secrets of everyone involved in this chronicle, and last, the texts which finally fell into his hands."[10] I feel a strong affinity with this description, which reflects the basic approach that I myself have followed in the process of researching and writing the particular story of the Covid-19 pandemic set out in these pages.

An often-forgotten aspect of the practice of reading is what is not read. "Hands up if about 20 months ago, you thought you would take advantage of the pandemic lockdown to do more reading," Stephanie Hogan writes in December 2021, "Now, hands up if those good intentions actually manifested in a stack of unread books on your bedside table."[11] This evidence of *intentions*, whether in a real stack or just a mental bookcase of "should" reads, points toward the role of reading as a space for possibilities in an individual's life – a series of possible ways in which life can be imagined as one or another kind of self-contained world that draws together diverse, fragmentary, and contradictory realities of lived experience into a type of narrative. The idea of such an engagement with the possible is enough for many of us to want to read a given book, many books in fact, yet the pause drains us of the desire or will to realize all these possibilities, leaving us a stack of the unread (*un*possible). If what we are reading speaks to a(n) (re)imagining of the present, this *stack of unread books* can be said to address the unimaginability of a future in the pandemic.

THE PAUSE

Pandemic Pedagogy

In fall 2022, as most classes at my university return to in-person teaching, I was acutely aware of how meaningful this dynamic was for me and the majority of my students. The fact of being in the same room together, of talking with individuals and not at screens, the sense of overall presence that was so lacking in online experiences, being face to face felt truly real. I met students for the first time that I had been teaching for the last two years, even failing to recognize some who consistently turned their cameras on for online class – which was surreal. We often forget how much information all of our senses absorb in person, which is severely limited when the exchange is flattened onto a digital screen.

When the lockdown went into effect in March 2020, it was about three weeks before the end of the winter semester, which meant that – after a pause week – I was, along with most professors, required to teach the remaining classes remotely. This move to complete online delivery was difficult in itself, yet the hardest part was addressing the temporal problem that came with this shift, the sudden need to accommodate not only synchronous virtual experiences but also asynchronous ones as well. In her article "Teaching Art Online under Covid-19," adjunct professor of visual art Kaitlin Pomerantz describes what was for many a common situation:

In the final days of spring "break"-turned-Covid-prep marathon and (uncompensated) online professional

116

Asynchronicity

development crash course, I watched colleagues – about 30 of whom I am in urgent dialogue with as we tried to make sense of the sparse and wires-crossed information coming from our schools – brainstorm and trouble shoot their own teaching challenges and provide emotional support, suggestions, hope, and sense to each other and to students. We navigated and participated in newly created online resource share groups, such as Facebook's "Online Art & Design Studio Instruction in the Age of 'Social Distancing,'" scoured open-source documents, researched differences between online platforms, learned about synchronous and asynchronous teaching models, scrapped our old syllabi and started to imagine new ones.[12]

While practice-based education proved particularly difficult to translate into an online format, all teaching suffered to various degrees as many practices that had been easy in person, sometimes done without having to think about them, suddenly became hyperconscious activities that took a lot of effort to accomplish.

It is important that we make the distinction between synchronous and asynchronous teaching clear. By synchronous, I mean the way material is delivered and received at the same time, which is possible even remotely through live streaming; when I lecture on Yam Lau's video *Covid Life* (2020), I speak about the work and show visuals, which students experience in the moment of presentation, and anyone who is absent misses out. In this mode, there is a shared space-time, either literally in person or live online. This is quite different from asynchronous teaching in which material is presented at one time but received at another, often several others, since each student can experience the material whenever they choose; here I lecture on Yam Lau's *Covid Life*, recording what I say and show, which is posted for students to watch by themselves when they want. In this mode, the space-time is fragmented, disjunctive, with little to no relation between the time of presentation and that of reception. Students even had a tendency to pause lectures and continue them on a different day. If synchronous is like a live event or program on television, which starts at one particular time and ends at another, asynchronous is closer to streaming in which one can determine one's own temporal relation with the event.

Another important distinction to make is between traditional online instruction and what is referred to as emergency remote teaching (ERT). "One prominent difference is the level of advance preparation each affords: while ERT is unexpected and unplanned, traditional online learning is deliberate and 'well-planned.'"[13] It is understood that the limitations of this mode of delivery have been fully considered in the process of planning a course or other instruction for online education, the benefits of which, such as the ability to study at a distance and while working full time, outweigh the potential losses. Such a situation is completely different from the sudden shift to online teaching that took place as a result of the Covid-19 pandemic, in which the existing in-person model was no longer

Asynchronicity

possible and an alternative needed to be instituted immediately. This "need to 'just get it online' is in direct contradiction to the time and effort normally dedicated to developing a quality course. Online courses created in this way should not be mistaken for long-term solutions but accepted as a temporary solution to an immediate problem."[14]

Asynchronous experience, while at times necessary during the pandemic, deprived many people of their sense of presence in time, and space, and community, their unique existence in the place where they happened to be. As Shawn Micallef writes: "Apart from the teaching itself, each classroom is its own universe, with its own culture and atmosphere. Students all have their usual seats and it becomes familiar human geography. That intimacy is lost online."[15] Such existential limitations to one's sense of being in the world have caused practical and psychological problems that, on the level of education, manifest as a feeling of being paused even while things continue to move forward – an effect that we have seen continue into 2023, well after the reinstitution of in-person education. Yet in a different way, pausing can be used to resist the "newly imposed condition of constant availability and connectivity enabled by the infinite spread of online teaching and research technologies during the Covid-19 pandemic."[16] Part of my fascination with the condition of asynchronicity is the way this mode of temporality contains and is contained by the pause. It is the asynchronous experience, most visible within educational situations, that powerfully alludes to the human limits of imagining a pandemic.

THE PAUSE

Zoom

One of the more astonishing changes to take place with the pandemic was the implementation of video-based communications on a mass scale, becoming a replacement for many interactions that would normally have taken place in person. The idea of conducting all of my university duties virtually, from teaching to faculty meetings to graduate supervision and defences, would have been inconceivable for me and many professors before Covid-19. "Now we hide ourselves behind the screens, taking online classes, joining Teams meetings and like us having this virtual seminar via Zoom today," Jiang Jiehong states in a discussion with Xiang Biao in June 2020:

> With absolutely no chance of face-to-face meetings and relying purely on these digital platforms, I am not sure whether technology has really connected us or actually distanced us. The current distance between you and me is probably approximately 65 miles – from Birmingham to Oxford, a 1-hour drive. But what kind of distance is it between us now, some 20 inches away from our screen? Of course not, it is immeasurable.[17]

Returning to in-person teaching in 2022, the extent of what had been lost in and through these online engagements, the realities of the *immeasurable distance* Jiang Jiehong is referring to, has and continues to become increasingly obvious. Yet it would be a mistake to simply minimize the benefits of this shift, which aided the social distancing required to limit the spread of the

120

Asynchronicity

"Does everyone understand?" teaching with Zoom meme.

virus while at the same time allowing many activities to continue that otherwise could not have.

Looking back at the Spanish flu, as with pandemics before it, the need to isolate and quarantine meant that much of everyday life was completely stopped for the duration of the outbreak. As Elizabeth Outka writes in *Viral Modernism: The Influenza Pandemic and Interwar Literature*, "In most communities, the schools, theaters, churches, and factories were all shut down, and many public services simply stopped. Too many people were ill – or taking care of the ill – to keep services running."[18] To be a professor or student at this time meant not attending classes at all, not doing assignments, and in fact literally not moving forward with one's career or education, which resumed only after the pandemic subsided. This is what happened with Isaac Newton, who was sent home from Cambridge for about two years during the Great Plague of London; although he continued his research, the progression of his academic career was put on hold for this time. The fact that I was able to continue teaching and students were able to continue studying while in isolation is significant, both practically and psychically. While many people have expressed their belief that they have lost the last two years of their lives, in truth more of this "life" was available to us during the pause because of these video-communications technologies that allowed individuals to be *present* even while in isolation.

Adjusting to emergency remote communications meant also adjusting to the online existence that accompanies it, with its advantages and perils. On the one hand, such an existence was the only option during the lockdowns and subsequent public restrictions. Even as this necessity subsided, the change that was brought about through the use of these online platforms has, at least in the short term, had a significant impact on how workspaces and work schedules are conceived. A 2022 study in the US "showed that only 3% of white-collar employees prefer to work in the office five days a week, and 86% want to work from home at least two days a week."[19] The common

Asynchronicity

use of video-based communications to work remotely during the first years of the pandemic opened up what some have called the "digital Zoom revolution," which has changed our societal understandings of workspaces and work schedules exponentially. Addressing these changes in higher education institutions in South Africa and Ghana, researchers Samuel Amponsah, Michael M. van Wyk, and Michael Kojo Kolugu note that, in the words of one participant in their study, engaging with digital video-conferencing platforms "had a positive impact on my knowledge of how to use these and other online tools."[20] On the other hand, the negative effects of this form of virtual communication have been well documented, relating to what are key losses in experience. This includes the phenomenon of "Zoom fatigue," which directly speaks to the psychological exhaustion accompanying excess virtual, screen-based engagements that allow communication but fundamentally lack (human) connection – in both synchronous and asynchronous contexts.[21]

The way things have manifested within this virtual space is particularly telling, defining a specific quality of the pause as it has developed through the pandemic. The final day before my university officially closed in response to Covid-19, I participated in one of a very few graduate defences that would take place in person – the committee meeting, asking the candidate questions, and deciding the outcome of this process. Immediately following this experience, all defences were made asynchronous – the committee members reading the thesis separately and submitting reports of their assessment that were given to the student, along with a decision about their degree. While online synchronous defences have become more common, there was something anticlimactic and even disheartening about this virtual practice, most notably the lack of shared presence in space and time. What was lost in this was the natural dialogue, the interpersonal discussion and exchanges that happen when people are together, which are the vital parts of such defences.

"Zoom defences" were part of a larger societal trend, which included "Zoom weddings," "Zoom graduations," and "Zoom funerals," among other variants. While I appreciate the desire to continue practising these "normal" activities, it is a mistake to treat the shift online as anything more than a loose translation. In April 2020, Bifo wrote: "What we experience in these weeks is a huge expansion of the time spent online, and it couldn't be otherwise because the emotional, productive, educational relationships must be transferred to the sphere in which one can not touch nor conjoin. Any sociality that is not purely connective ceases to exist."[22] Life itself, in terms of lived experience (or an experience of living) in this pause, has been profoundly asynchronous, defined by a collective sense of waiting – waiting to find out the full extent of the virus, waiting for vaccines, waiting for the restrictions to subside, waiting to understand what has happened, waiting for supply chains to normalize, waiting for the normal to return, waiting to feel "normal" again. Part of experiencing the pause has been this overwhelming need to not exist in the time of pandemic and instead wait for the world to return, to be returned to us.

Asynchronicity

Life Asynchronous

In a September 2022 article in *The Guardian*, Stephen Burgen discusses plans by Spain to offer "digital nomad" visas that would allow people from "outside the European Economic Area" who are "able to demonstrate that they have been working remotely for at least a year" to live in the country, which provides a relatively low cost of living and added tax incentives.[23] Similar programs exist in countries around the world that target "remote workers," including one offered by Malaysia "that may become the first fully fledged digital nomad and remote worker pass to be offered in Southeast Asia."[24] The idea of living in a place that is literally divorced from one's work, which can be done from "anywhere," perfectly follows the logic of the pandemic. One of the lessons we seem to be trying to take from living through Covid-19 is that work, or specific types of work, does not necessarily require one to go *to* work. This in turn means one can have a life in itself that simply includes moments when work happens – abstractly, through the medium of the computer or similar device. While this has been a possibility for many years, notably for any job that is or can be primarily done through a computer, the necessity of working from a distance during the pandemic has been an impetus for truly exploring this possibility. The temporary disconnection of work from a specified working space or place is now being considered as a possible long-term way of living, in which one's work no longer needs to dictate the spatial and temporal realities of one's existence.

THE PAUSE

Perhaps this is part of what is meant when people refer to the "new normal" that emerges with the (so-called) end of the pandemic, or at least the end of specific waves or chapters of the pandemic. "Normal will never come back," Bifo boldly declares when thinking about a post-lockdown state, which can also be applied to the rest of the pandemic to date: "What will happen in the aftermath has not yet been determined, and is not predictable."[25] Who could have predicted the need for "digital nomad" visas, the fact that the pandemic would bring about such problems with global supply chains – that the pandemic would make "clear that the supply chain *is* the society"[26] – or the fact that students whose primary social engagements are online would have such an intense desire to return to in-person education? The question of the "normal" is tied to the flattening of experience, both actual and possible, with the sense of timelessness it implies. Such a profane purgatory, the most negative quality of the pause, is sustained in and through the temporal hesitations of an asynchronous life.

When teaching my university courses online, I always included a live check-in once a week, which served to keep the students grounded and provide much-needed structure to an otherwise temporally ambiguous semester. While the goal was to allow students a chance to ask questions about the readings and discuss topics related to the progression of the course, the fact that each of us were streaming live from our residences also meant experiencing glimpses of each other's private lives and sharing in odd moments of distraction and interruption. Along with these synchronous meetings, I would post videos of the

126

Asynchronicity

weekly lectures, which meant that each student could watch when they wanted and how they wanted, which is understood as a mostly positive feature of asynchronous learning. Yet, in my experience, this lack of structure led to students failing to know how to "experience" the material. In person, they would have to sit and listen to a lecture, taking notes on those ideas that seemed important and that they were able to catch – missing some of what is said and taught is part of the process of learning. With video, students have ultimate choice, being able to play the lecture at normal speed or double speed (as many admitted to me they did), and never having to miss a single word because they can pause and replay at will; in fact, several students told me they actively attempted to take notes on every single thing I said, demonstrating no desire or ability to distinguish between important and unimportant ideas. As asynchronous, such an experience is deprived of a given sense of time that instead is treated as a flattened temporality, as simultaneous, which is overwhelming.

Experiences of time within the pause are particularly relative, if not in many cases quite voluntary or accidental. One can be rushed and bored at the same time, which makes it difficult to feel any sense of necessity to get things done – we find ourselves out of sync with our own lives, even in the process of living them. This asynchronous sensibility pressures us on very personal and subjective levels, making us restless in our very experience of ourselves, exhausting the ways in which we exist. I want to position this sensibility within what Elizabeth Outka will term "narrative vertigo":

THE PAUSE

Our pandemic narrative remains mired in uncertainty, repetition, and uneven losses and gains, a kind of narrative vertigo that means we don't know where we are in the timeline or what characters we are playing. We certainly don't know the ending. Or what happens next. Or whether there will be an endless number of mind-numbing sequels after Omicron.[27]

Extending this, I believe the pause represents a loss of temporal balance in which the timeline of our pandemic narrative has been made to feel as if it is not happening *in* time – or, perhaps more accurately, as if time is not necessarily happening in the pandemic. The pause invites each of us individually to re-experience time, which appears somewhat the same as outside the pandemic, but is not.

On Abstraction, Boredom, and Pausing

Pause.
— Georges Perec[1]

Covid Life

This chronicle is drawing to a close. It is time for me to admit that at the beginning of the pandemic I really did not take Covid-19 seriously, assuming, like many others, that the situation was not as bad as it seemed. When my university announced it would be closed from 13 March until 24 April 2020 it felt like an overreaction – the truth, that it would not open up fully again until 2022 with the return of in person classes, that we would have to endure a series of lockdowns and years of restrictions, would have sounded ludicrous. At that early stage, the reality of the pandemic was for me literally unimaginable. In fact, even now, in 2023, I am not sure if I have even managed to imagine the pandemic in the right way (or if it is even possible to do so). "Words are powerless against the Plague," one commentator writes when discussing Camus's novel, "it demands action. Not spectacular action with brilliant victories, but modest efforts, tirelessly repeated from day to day."

THE PAUSE

Experiencing the pandemic is not, as one might expect from the outside, a spectacular encounter with a pestilence that dramatically appears and disappears "like the devil in Germanic legends,"[2] but instead is an almost nondescript stoppage or gap within life, a pause in humanity's sense of its own existence.

"Apparently, nothing had changed": Camus describes the social atmosphere near the beginning of the plague in Oran, although such a sentiment can also be used to characterize various moments throughout the Covid-19 pandemic, including its (so-called) end.[3] Georges Perec makes a similar observation in his book *An Attempt at Exhausting a Place in Paris* when addressing his encounter with Place Saint-Sulpice at the start of his second day: "What has changed since yesterday? At first sight, it's really the same."[4] One of the main qualities I appreciate about Perec's exercises of looking is the way he forces himself to pay attention to the ordinary everyday elements of life in a particular place or through a precise way of thinking, consciously observing "events" that everyone else is more than likely to ignore. At numerous points in the narrative, he even articulates moments of *pause*, which exist as stand-alone conditions outside the narration of the scene yet are vital to its psychological reception. And this is an aspect of the current pandemic that is powerfully and at times painfully present, the experience of the pause as both a personal and existential interruption in the perceptual flow of people's lives.

Yam Lau shares his own vision of this experience in an artwork created in 2020 aptly titled *Covid Life*. Starting with a linear grid of black lines on a white background, a black and white video of clouds reflected in water slowly fades into view, ac-

On Abstraction, Boredom, and Pausing

companied by subtle sounds of nature. But the abstraction of the grid remains, imposed overtop the scene. Just past the halfway point, the layered sounds of media reports on the pandemic emerge, while the grid and reflections begin to blur, becoming a mass of abstracted forms; which come back into focus as the news reports fade away, followed by the reflections of clouds in water fading back into a white screen and grid. I am struck by the imposition of the grid, which is reminiscent of the grid works by modernist artist Agnes Martin – one of Yam Lau's "artist heroes." Yet his use is less geometric and more about the occurrence of an abstractness that stands between us and the representations of the world he (re)presents. "To fight against abstraction," Camus's narrator tells us, "You had to resemble it a little."[5] *Covid Life* accepts this struggle in and through the abstractness of the grid, which embraces the missed memories of life under pandemic by mis-apprehending an abstract moment of imperfection.

Yam Lau, *Covid Life* (still), 2022.

In truth, the pandemic is an abstraction, and the pause is the subjective manifestation of this abstraction. Which, following Malabou's logic of *quarantine within the quarantine*, we might articulate in terms of a *pause within the pause*. Here we can see the crisis of imagination as a consequence of confronting, avoiding, or trying to make sense of this existential abstraction.

Relational Paralysis

"The effect of the virus is not linked to the number of people it kills," Bifo writes in March 2020. "The effect of the virus lies in the relational paralysis it is spreading."[6] While he uses this phrase only once in his three diaries (of psycho-deflation), the concept of "paralysis" appears in a number of his writings, including in the books *Futurability* and *Breathing*. In both, the idea of paralysis is employed when discussing the social body, an approach that easily lends itself to his critical engagement with the pandemic. In fact, it could even be argued that for Bifo the experience of Covid-19 is tied to a larger need to re-define the social body, which is grounded in and through the limits imposed by neoliberal capitalist structures, limits we often-times fail to even recognize as such but which cannot be ignored in times of crisis. Bifo described the global revolts that took place in the last months of 2019 as "a sort of convulsion of the worldwide social body," which "resulted in a collapse." But, he writes in early May 2022, "now we are in something like a paralysis that follows collapse. What we are feeling now is the fear of contagion, of boredom, and of the world that we'll find

On Abstraction, Boredom, and Pausing

when we'll be allowed to go out again."[7] Paralysis in this understanding is a lack or failure of functionality in relation to the social body, a social bodily collapse (to relate it more closely to the term's Latin roots), which collectively is unable to properly respond or move forward, life becoming socially dis-abled.

Bifo is particularly invested in the psychological effects of this paralysis, which defines the condition of "psycho-deflation," the subtitle for his Covid-19 diaries. As he states, "Psychological energy is sapped from the social body, imagination slows, and the collective body is paralyzed."[8] This *sapping* of psychological energy within the pandemic is a deflationary process in which individuals feel drained, without a sense of vitality or purpose, perpetually unable to find meaning in life or lived experience. One of the key results of this lack is the slowing of imagination. As Camus highlights, it is the question of the limits of imagination that is foregrounded during pandemics, challenging people to think at a scale beyond the human. Bifo is describing the other side of this limitation, in which the individual is psychically paralyzed through this failure of imagination that is also a *paralysis* on the level of social relations. This idea of relational paralysis describes a renouncing or abandoning of psychological expectations, especially at the level of the social body (*communal sense*), due to the prolonged internalization of fear during the pandemic.

In their text "Care for the People in Times of Pandemic: Collective Reflections to Overcome Uncertainty, Essays to Avoid Inhabiting Impotence," the Plurinational and Popular Women's Parliament and the Feminist Organisations of Ecuador discuss approaches for collectively thinking through the present care crisis. "It is time to think of ourselves as part of something broader, more humble, empathic. Put life in the center and understand that no life is worth more than another, that we all need lives of dignity and freedom from violence, as the indigenous peoples have always taught us," they write, noting that "Bifo lucidly named this emergency: relational paralysis."[9] This use of Bifo's phrase calls attention to the question of how to understand life at a time when life is itself a question, when the relations between human beings, as well as the human relations to all other beings in the world, are paralyzed. On the one hand, "the #StayHome has paused the voracious and destructive logic of capitalism, temporarily improving life on the planet." On the other hand, such a pausing necessarily raises questions: "How then do we imagine care, if to appease contagion we require a suspension of relations? How do we politicize physical distance and confinement? ... Which memories do we belong to, which do we honor?"[10]

On 10 November 2022 – as the question of bringing back the mask mandates in Canada was being debated in the media – I attended a talk at the Gardiner Museum in Toronto, given by my friend the curator and writer Maya Wilson-Sánchez, about her curated exhibition *Replicas and Reunions: Ancient and Contemporary Ceramics from Ecuador*. Born in Ecuador, Maya explored the relationships among Ecuadorian ceramic objects in the museum's collection and a series of new "copies," a "body of work by Quito-based artist Pamela Cevallos and five collaborators from the rural coastal town of La Pila: Andrés López, Genaro López, Daniel Mezones, Javier Rivera, and Guillermo Quijije."[11] In the main display, ceramic figures from the collec-

On Abstraction, Boredom, and Pausing

tion were paired with their contemporary doppelgangers, the two positioned not addressing the viewer but instead standing looking at each other. In a time of continuing forms of relational paralysis, Maya shares a creative vision of the social body through the imaginings and memories captured in relations among cultural objects of different times and spaces.

Empty Spaces of the World

"The exhibition is now on pause, sitting still in a closed gallery," Magda Sawon writes about Serkan Özkaya's *Left Is Right, Down Is Up* after shutting Postmasters Gallery in early March 2020.[12] Given the situation at that moment, Sawon's decision to install the show is significant because it demonstrates a belief in the importance of art even at the threshold of pandemic. Her act reflects a statement by art critic Jason Farago: "In times of adversity, we look to art to give form to chaos."[13] Sawon's choice of the specific word "pause" reflects the reality of the act as she saw it, not the stopping or closing of the exhibition, not even its cancellation – some galleries simply did not install shows until after the spaces reopened – but rather allowing the installation to exist, to occupy the space of the gallery, even though the (human) experience of it had to temporarily be put on hold. Yet, this is more than simply the pushing of a *pause button*, with its built-in assumption of un-pausing and a return to normal. Instead, this confrontation with the empty gallery is, I argue, an embracing of Bifo's concept of relational paralysis – or what I have called the pause.

It is fascinating to imagine all the empty spaces around the world that punctuated the summer 2020 lockdowns: restaurants with no diners, stores with no shoppers, theatres and arenas without spectators, museums and galleries without viewers. The vision of emptied parking lots still emotionally captures the experience of this (anthropaused) moment as I remember it. Bifo describes the unnerving quietness of life in Italy: "The noisy city is silent, the schools are closed, the theatres closed. No students around, no tourists. Travel agencies are cancelling entire regions from the map."[14] Photographs document the absence of people in the typically well-populated Piazza Navona in Rome and Piazza del Duomo in Florence, imagery that resists the human at a foundational level. This is most apparent in the particularly haunting scene of Pope Francis delivering the *Urbi* and *Orbi* ("To the City and To the World") prayer in an empty St Peter's Square at the Vatican on 27 March. As one journalist wrote about the event: "In yet another surreal sight to emerge from the Covid-19 coronavirus pandemic, Pope Francis on Friday delivered a blessing from a strikingly deserted St Peter's Square."[15] Standing in this space in spring 2022, even with some people around, a sense of the existential lack pictured in the image of Pope Francis was still very much present.

Emptiness became profound inside the pandemic. In 2020, there were numerous insightful events centring on this question of the world being emptied, specifically of human presence – an anthropocentric conceit, but reflective of human reality nonetheless. In her interview with Jiang Jiehong, singer and sound artist Zhu Zheqin (Dadawa) notes three examples: "At the beginning of February, Ryuichi Sakamoto held a live con-

On Abstraction, Boredom, and Pausing

Robert Fitterman in *Left Is Right, Down Is Up* at Postmasters Gallery, 11 July 2020.

cert in his house in New York; Chang Jing held a *guzheng* (a traditional Chinese instrument) performance on Bilibili in March; in April Andrea Bocelli held an astonishing online concert in the Milan Cathedral (*Duomo di Milano*) in Italy."[16] To these I add the empty gallery of *Left Is Right, Down Is Up*, in which the poet Robert Fitterman would give a talk with no audience; hockey games played without an audience – "it felt so bizarre-looking at the giant bowl that usually holds close to 20,000 sit completely empty"[17] – with fake crowd noises, making the entire experience quite abstract; the un-inhabited spaces of Yam Lau's *Covid Life*, which embraces this sense of abstractness. Even after the lockdowns ended and people re-entered the world, this emptiness seems to have continued to haunt life under the spectre of Covid-19.

In the case of museum and gallery exhibitions, a number of particularly interesting strategies were employed in an attempt to negotiate this emptiness. Because of the lockdowns and restrictive measures, such exhibitionary spaces quickly moved their displays into the digital realm, developing and extending the capacities of existing websites by creating virtual walkthroughs, "viewing rooms," and other online spaces that allow engagement at a (social) distance. The Uffizi in Florence, for example, created an online tour of major works from their collection, which allowed the virtual viewer to "walk" around and see works from different angles. Another example is M+ in Hong Kong, which created video walk-throughs for the museum – "Sometimes I feel like I am working in a TV station," curator Pi Li stated in a June 2020 interview, "when I have been dragged to record various guided tours which are entirely made available on digital platforms."[18] In addition to the push to make collections and exhibitions available online, we witnessed a number of exhibitionary practices meant to present artwork to people who could not be present. One of the more innovative examples was the British art museum Hastings Contemporary, which offered "robot tours" of their exhibitions "using a mobile, Wi-Fi-enabled 'telepresence' device that prowls the gallery, sending a video stream back to viewers who stay isolated at home."[19] Here we see the robot in front of Lakwena Maciver's painting aptly titled *Nothing Can Separate Us* (2020). In each alternative mode of presentation, the focus is on an inaccessible or, for all intents and purposes, absent space that is re-presented as a hyper-presence.

Robot tour of Hastings Contemporary, April 2020.

While sharing this research on a 2022 conference panel wonderfully titled "Let's Get Digital," organized by my young colleagues and friends Elyse Longair and Jevi Peters, it became clear that with this shift to the digital realm there is a corresponding move from experience to information. One does not "experience" the work in a virtual walk-through or viewing room, but rather encounters the work as information that is gathered or acquired (in the abstract). I cannot imagine someone crying when looking at a work on the Uffizi website, even

THE PAUSE

though I have witnessed this on several occasions in the museum itself. Jiang Jiehong articulates this problematic when he states: "In an online exhibition, one can still 'see' and 'hear' the work but one will not have the bodily experience in the physical space, to pace back and forth, to look and to unlook, and to pause and to think."[20] It is the *bodily experience* that cannot be captured or translated online, the ability to *unlook* at something, as well as the importance of being able to *pause* and to *think* in and through the experience. This understanding is particularly relevant when engaging with the emptiness that informs much of pandemic experience, which too often has been reduced to mere information rather than appreciated in its material and psychological complexities.

Covid-Boredom

We began 2022 still in the midst of the pandemic: still social distancing, still wearing masks, still feeling as if life was on pause. These restrictions, as necessary as they were in limiting the spread of the virus, meant that most of us had been for the past few years living in a limited environment with limited activities to occupy ourselves, to satisfy our need for meaningful experiences. Yet social and cultural distractions, most notably the various forms of popular entertainment, proved inadequate. A number of people I spoke with at the time confessed that they had been unable to fully binge TV programs because it felt *pointless*. Even watching the news, which in times of crisis

140

On Abstraction, Boredom, and Pausing

can border on compulsion, has become quite literally monotonous as we are presented with the same basic stories, the same series of information and "facts" about the virus and its effects, the same fears and concerns, repeated over and over with only minor variations. This is why fake news and conspiracy theories thrived during key phases of the pandemic – because, according to communications theorist David Black, they are "more psychologically pleasing and convenient" than reality and they make "simpler sense than a complex phenomenon."[21] The repeated denial of even the possibility of meaningful experiences resulted in a profound sense of boredom directly related to living in the pandemic, a *Covid-boredom.*

This type of boredom is fundamentally tied to what is often referred to as FOMO, the *fear of missing out.* FOMO is defined as "a pervasive apprehension that others might be having rewarding experiences from which one is absent," notably "characterized by the desire to stay continually connected with what others are doing."[22] While this phenomenon predates Covid-19, the pandemic clearly heightened its effects, especially given the fact that FOMO is grounded within the unique relations experienced through social media communications and interactions. Individual activities take on increased significance when they are weighed against the loss of possible experiences people feel like they might have had if Covid-19 had not interrupted or affected their lives, or experiences others are perceived as having. Instead of preparing to apply for graduate schools in 2021, university student Darshina Dhunnoo notes: "I've kind of accepted that that's not going to happen."[23] This example is particularly significant for me since, as a professor, I have had numerous conversations about this exact issue, in which students express their fears of missing a year of their lives while, on social media, seeing the lives of other students moving forward.

The pandemic put much of life on hold, from work and education to medical procedures and travel. Decisions have been postponed and plans put off until after the pause, waiting for a post-pandemic state when life can be *un-paused*. Even after the world mostly opened back up in summer and fall 2022 – in fact, even in 2023, after we felt as though we had left Covid-19 behind – this fear of missing out remained a core drive for so many people who continued trying to make up for the sense of lost experiences by, in many cases, attempting to get too much "meaning" out of activities. And when this "meaning" fails to live up to or alleviate this perceived loss or lack, a common result has been Covid-boredom – an existential lassitude that deprives one of an ability to truly recognize or believe in having rewarding experiences. Yet, such an act of being bored does not stop one from engaging in apparently *pointless* activities, but instead encourages more and more of the same. In trying to solve the problem of our boredom, we add layers to the things we are already doing; if bingeing a TV program feels pointless, we start bingeing several programs simultaneously. We engage in *more* – more watching, more buying, more trying new things, more possibilities, more rethinking our lives – to hyper-stimulate ourselves. But the ironic effect of these added "experiences" seems to be more Covid-boredom.

During the pandemic, "boredom" has become a code word for any experience in which people feel disconnected, when life

On Abstraction, Boredom, and Pausing

appears meaningless or uninteresting. In his article "Is the Lockdown Making You Depressed, or Are You Just Bored?" Dr Richard Friedman distinguished between an expanded sense of boredom and the clinical diagnosis of depression, conditions that he believes are being confused in the current situation. He writes: "Being bored might feel intolerable, but, unlike clinical depression, it will never seriously impair your function or kill you."[24] The inability to distinguish between boredom and depression points to a larger problem of recognizing the difference between experiencing a lack of interest and an inability to experience interest at all. With Covid-boredom, our lack of interest is exaggerated to the point where it can feel as if the experience is impossible, an existential hell that can feel like, to use one commentator's phrasing, "a boring apocalypse."[25] Covid-boredom is the ultimate manifestation of the crisis of imagination during the pandemic.

In *Wuhan Diary*, Fang Fang writes: "And now, although we are no longer living in terror and the sadness has dissipated a bit, we must face an indescribable boredom and restlessness, along with endless waiting."[26] Here Fang nicely captures the sense in which Covid-boredom is the other side of an overarching anxiety about the pandemic and its consequences. Like the layers of stress and worry that have been felt throughout the world as we face the possibility of the pandemic lasting longer and longer, of "normalcy" getting further and further away from us, boredom with this reality is also layered. We must think of boredom in the pandemic not as a single experience, but rather as layers of experiences of being bored that together feel personally and even socially overwhelming. People are not simply bored but are bored with being bored, which is perhaps why some need to see and treat it as depression. But this Covid-boredom asks us important questions about the ways humanity thinks about life from inside a pandemic.

Re-imagining the Pause

In *States of Plague: Reading Albert Camus in a Pandemic*, Laura Marris writes: "Yet in the pandemic year, *The Plague* has been tested as a direct chronicle of illness and held its own. We have all, to some extent, become residents within its chapters."[27] At numerous times while reading Camus's novel, I have felt a synchronicity between the story he told and the narrative that has developed around Covid-19. The personalities and reactions of the characters often mirror the general types of views and responses people have had during the pandemic, from those who deny the existence of the illness or continue downplaying its severity to those who refuse to accept being quarantined or selfishly act without regard for the well-being of others. In the midst of the novel, Camus describes people pretending to engage in a variety of activities, from reading newspapers to listening to the radio, all in an attempt to contend with the "stifling boredom"[28] – the *indescribable boredom* that Fang Fang articulates (Friedman as well in his own way).

Yet, for me this connection with *The Plague* goes beyond becoming *residents within its chapters* and includes, to some extent, the ways people's changing relations with the pandemic are reflected in engagements with the material book itself.

On Abstraction, Boredom, and Pausing

During lockdowns, and at times when the virus and its effects were most obvious, was when Camus's novel appeared to be a *direct chronicle of illness*. At other times, when the pandemic was particularly surreal, when the experience was less direct and more abstract, it felt as if I was holding the book and looking at the words but not always being able to read them – pausing in an attempt to try to make sense of the story. At still other times, when the social distancing and mask mandates were lifted and many believed it was the "end" of the pandemic, I literally closed the book and put it back on my shelf only to go back and take it down, put it back and take it down again. As it turned out, I have remained unsure if I still need this chronicle or not – if, we might say, life is in fact still inhabiting or dwelling in those pages.

And that is where we are as I (attempt to) close out my own *chronicle*, with a pandemic that appears to be over even while it continues to persist. In fact, a previous title for this final chapter was "It's Over, But It's Not Over," an attempt to capture the extreme ambiguity of the moment. Yet, defining the parameters of this "moment," which has been going on far longer than many expected, has proven difficult. While some early accounts optimistically proposed that the virus could be "cured" by the end of 2020, others suggested that we might be living with this coronavirus for at least the near future, with Covid-19 entering "into long-term circulation alongside the other human betacoronaviruses, possibly in annual, biennial, or sporadic patterns over the next five years."[29] In journalist Teena Thacker's 2022 article "Pandemic Headed for a Long Pause, but Not the End, Warn Experts," she quotes Anurag Agrawal, director at the CSIR Institute of Genomics and Integrative Biology, who succinctly states: "A pause maybe, but not the end."[30]

This *long pause*, which has also been called the *great pause* – or, as I have suggested, a *pause within the pause* – is an extended state of suspension that invites questions of what will come after, especially when the concept of an "end" feels impossible. One solution was to speculate about the post-pandemic, which started as early as 2021 – Benjamin Bratton's *The Revenge of the Real: Politics for a Post-Pandemic World* being an ideal example. Here we look past the pandemic's end even as we contend with a number of variants that have continued to plague us into 2023. I appreciate the honesty of Kim Wong-Shing, when she writes at the beginning of her December 2021 article:

> In April 2021, I pitched a story idea to my editors: "How to cope with post-pandemic anxiety." As vaccines became widely available, I pictured parties with no masks, handshakes with no fear and all the other markers of a world going back to "normal." In this imminent post-pandemic future, I thought my biggest challenge would be re-adjusting to life outside my cocoon. Half a year and several new Covid variants later, it has become clear that the very concept of "post-pandemic" requires re-examining. For starters, it's not clear what it means for a pandemic to end – even scientists disagree on where to draw the line.[31]

Even looking to past pandemics for some sense of how an "end" might look only seems to add to this uncertainty. As the

On Abstraction, Boredom, and Pausing

title of Eleanor Cummins's article nicely articulates, "The Story of the Spanish Flu Ended Before the Virus Did. The Same Is Happening with the Covid Pandemic" (March 2022). She describes this condition as *narrative vertigo*, a concept put forward by Elizabeth Outka, who writes: "Historical accounts can rarely capture the experience of narrative vertigo, the dizzying sense of scrambling for traction in midair before a finished story is possible."[32] But, as I stated from the outset, my aim has not been in writing a "finished story" of the pandemic.

The notion of *the pause* that I have put forward in this book defines not an end but rather its impossibility. It attempts to embrace the ambiguity of the Covid-19 pandemic, not simply by assigning or denying meaning to given events and realities, but instead by accepting that meaning inside pandemic conditions is never a fixed experience and therefore must always be imagined and re-imagined. We return to the idea of imagination, so important to Camus's understanding of plagues, because this is what pausing opens up for us – the ability to *look and to unlook, and to pause and to think.* What happens when life stops but does not *stop*, when there is a break in existence even while the realities of *existing* continue? Rather than a single moment or state, the pause defines a day-to-day continuum of repeated experiences that, even when different, even when they have changed over the course of the pandemic, are somehow still experienced as the same. Amid this ambiguity, I have devoted myself, within these pages, to becoming a historian of what has no history.

Pause.

Notes

Preface

1 Georges Perec, *An Attempt at Exhausting a Place in Paris*, trans. Marc Lowenthal (Cambridge: Wakefield Press, 2010), 17.
2 Teresa Wright, "Will 2023 Be the Year COVID-19 Becomes Endemic in Canada? Experts Weigh In," *Global News*, 1 January 2023 [6:00 am], https://globalnews.ca/news/9370959/covid-endemic-2023-experts.
3 Isaac Bogoch, quoted in ibid.
4 Peter Conlin, "Time Lapse Interview with J.J. Haladyn on Boredom and Pausing," *Time Lapse*, Youtube, 30 June 2022, https://www.youtube.com/watch?v=cxeN6gBCaOo.

Acknowledgments

1 Georges Perec, *An Attempt at Exhausting a Place in Paris*, trans. Marc Lowenthal (Cambridge: Wakefield Press, 2010), 37.

Covid-19 and the Crisis of Imagination

1 Georges Perec, *An Attempt at Exhausting a Place in Paris*, trans. Marc Lowenthal (Cambridge: Wakefield Press, 2010), 42.
2 Magda Sawon, "How to Experience 'Experience Art' in a Pandemic – A Modest Proposal," press release, reprinted in *Left Is Right, Down Is Up: Serkan Özkaya and Joseph Beuys* (exhibition catalogue) (Postmasters Gallery, n.d. [circa 2021]), n.p.

NOTES TO PAGES 7–13

3 Li Lin to Jiang Jiehong, "In Fashion at Home," in *The Otherness of the Everyday: Twelve Conversations from the Chinese Art World during the Covid-19 Pandemic*, ed. Jiang Jiehong (Bristol: Intellect, 2021), 103.

4 Catherine Malabou, "To Quarantine from Quarantine: Rousseau, Robinson Crusoe, and 'I,'" *Critical Inquiry Blog*, 23 March 2020, https://critinq.wordpress.com/2020/03/23/to-quarantine-from-quarantine-rousseau-robinson-crusoe-and-i/.

5 Christian W. McMillen, *Pandemics: A Very Short Introduction* (New York: Oxford University Press, 2016), 18.

6 Jean-Jacques Rousseau, *Confessions*, trans. P.N. Furbank (New York: Everyman's Library, 1992), 270.

7 Thucydides, *The Peloponnesian War*, trans. Martin Hammond (Oxford: Oxford University Press, 2009), 97.

8 Procopius, *History of the Wars*, vol. 1 (*The Persian War*), trans. H.B. Dewing, Loeb Classical Library (Cambridge: Harvard University Press, 1914), 452.

9 See Gérard Chouin, "Reflections on Plague in African History (14th–19th c.)," *Afriques: Débats, méthodes et terrains d'histoire* 9 (2018): https://journals.openedition.org/afriques/2228.

10 Thomas E. Keys, "The Plague in Literature," *Bulletin of the Medical Library Association* 32 (1944): 52.

11 Frances Blackman, letter to George Lee, 9 November 1881; reproduced in "Smallpox 1881," *Honoring Native Ancestors*, 15 August 2019, honoringnativeancestors.blogspot.com/2019/08/smallpox-1881.html.

12 Lutiant LaVoye, quoted in Lili Loofbourow, "'The First One That Died Sure Unnerved Me': What a Mordantly Funny Letter from the 1918 Pandemic Says about 2020," *Slate Magazine*, 1 May 2020, https://slate.com/news-and-politics/2020/05/1918-flu-pandemic-nurse-letter.html.

13 Alexandra Alter, "Publishers Snap Up Corona Books, from Case Studies to Plague Poetry," *New York Times*, 18 May 2020, https://www.nytimes.com/2020/05/18/books/coronavirus-books-publishing.html.

NOTES TO PAGES 14–20

14 Penelope Ironstone and Greg Bird, "Editorial Introduction: Writing in the Midst of the Covid-19 Pandemic: From Vulnerability to Solidarity," *Topia: Canadian Journal of Cultural Studies* (Covid-19 Essays, 2020): https://www.utpjournals.press/jour nals/topia/covid-19-essays.

15 John Paul Ricco, "On Ways of Living in the Midst of the Covid-19 Global Pandemic (Three Brief Meditations)," *Topia* (Covid-19 Essays, 2020): https://www.utpjournals.press/journals/topia/covid-19-essays/on-ways-of-living-in-the-midst-of-the-covie-19-global-pandemic?

16 Fang Fang, *Wuhan Diary: Dispatches from a Quarantined City*, trans. Michael Berry (Toronto: Harper Collins, 2020), Apple eBook. Previous and following quotations are from the same source.

17 Giorgio Agamben, "The State of Exception Provoked by an Unmotivated Emergency," *Positions*, 26 February 2020, http://positionswebsite.org/giorgio-agamben-the-state-of-exception-provoked-by-an-unmotivated-emergency/.

18 Giorgio Agamben, foreword to *Where Are We Now? The Epidemic as Politics*, trans. Valeria Dani (London: Eris, 2021), 7.

19 Scott McLemee, "A Present of Things Past," *Inside Higher ED*, 27 May 2022, https://www.insidehighered.com/views/2022/05/27/roundup-fall-2022-books-cold-war-and-covid.

20 Albert Camus, *The Plague*, trans. Laura Marris (New York: Vintage Books, 2022), 41.

21 Ibid., 6.

22 Albert Camus, *The Plague*, trans. Robin Buss (New York: Penguin Books, 2013), 8.

23 Alice Kaplan and Laura Marris, *States of Plague: Reading Albert Camus in a Pandemic* (Chicago: University of Chicago Press, 2022), 3.

24 Jacqueline Rose, "'The Plague': Pointing the Finger," *London Review of Books* 42, no. 9 (May 2020): 3.

151

NOTES TO PAGES 21–7

Air

1 Georges Perec, *An Attempt at Exhausting a Place in Paris*, trans. Marc Lowenthal (Cambridge: Wakefield Press, 2010), 31.

2 David Hopkins, "Marcel Duchamp's *50cc of Paris Air*: Dada, Dissemination and Contagion," presented at "Duchamp Accelerated" International Symposium, OCAD University, Toronto, 7–8 March 2020.

3 Centers for Disease Control and Prevention, "Symptoms of Covid-19," CDC website, 22 March 2022 (updated version), https://www.cdc.gov/coronavirus/2019-ncov/symptoms-testing/symptoms.html.

4 Mayo Clinic, "Coronavirus Disease 2019 (COVID-19): Symptoms and Causes," Mayo Clinic website (accessed 17 June 2023), https://www.mayoclinic.org/diseases-conditions/coronavirus/symptoms-causes/syc-20479963.

5 Debora Mackenzie, "Covid-19: Why Won't the WHO Officially Declare a Coronavirus Pandemic?" *New Scientist*, 26 February 2020, updated 11 March 2020, https://www.newscientist.com/article/2235342-covid-19-why-wont-the-who-officially-declare-a-coronavirus-pandemic.

6 Saba Aziz, "'Far from Over': What Past Pandemics Can Tell Us about Ending Covid-19," *Global News*, 11 March 2022, https://globalnews.ca/news/8671295/covid-versus-past-pandemics-3rd-year.

7 Fred Khumalo, "Let's Run the Voodoo Down!" in *Lockdown Extended: Corona Chronicles*, ed. Melinda Ferguson (Cape Town: Melinda Ferguson Books, 2020), Apple eBook.

8 McMillen, *Pandemics*, 89.

9 David Hume, *An Enquiry concerning Human Reason* (Oxford: Oxford University Press, 2008), 26.

10 Ibid., 24.

11 Khumalo, "Let's Run the Voodoo Down!"

12 Elisabeth Stelson, "Covid and Camus: Reflections on *The Plague*, Collective Experience, and Qualitative Inquiry during a Pandemic," *Qualitative Social Work* 20, nos. 1–2 (2021): 42.

152

NOTES TO PAGES 28–34

13 Yam Lau, "Duchamp and the Play of Distances," presented at "Duchamp Accelerated" International Symposium, OCAD University, Toronto, 7–8 March 2020.

14 Allison McGeer, quoted in Ivan Semeniuk, "Scientists Look for Signs of Air Transmission of Covid-19," *The Globe and Mail*, 2 April 2020, https://www.theglobeandmail.com/canada/article-scientists-look-for-signs-of-air-transmission-of-covid-19/. See also Elizabeth L. Anderson, Paul Turnham, John R. Griffin, and Chester C. Clarke, "Consideration of the Aerosol Transmission for Covid-19 and Public Health," *Risk Analysis* 40, no. 5 (2020): https://doi.org/10.1111/risa.13500.

15 Hannah Arendt, *The Origins of Totalitarianism* (Orlando: Harcourt, 2001), 290.

16 Achille Mbembe, "The Universal Right to Breathe," trans. Carolyn Shread, *Critical Inquiry* 47 (Winter 2021): S61–2.

17 Ibid., S61.

18 Jelani Cobb, "The Death of George Floyd, in Context," *New Yorker*, 28 May 2020, https://www.newyorker.com/news/daily-comment/the-death-of-george-floyd-in-context.

19 Melina Abdullah, quoted in William Roberts, "George Floyd Two Years On: Some Accountability but Killings Go On," *Al Jazeera*, 25 May 2022, https://www.aljazeera.com/news/2022/5/25/george-floyd-two-years-on-some-accountability-but-killings-go-on.

20 Cobb, "The Death of George Floyd."

21 Melvin L. Rogers, "We Should Be Afraid, but Not of Protesters," in *The Politics of Care: From Covid-19 to Black Lives Matter*, eds. Gregg Gonsalves and Amy Kapczynski (New York: Verso, 2020), 181. See also Ed Pilkington, "Black Americans Dying of Covid-19 at Three Times the Rate of White People," *The Guardian*, 20 May 2020, https://www.theguardian.com/world/2020/may/20/black-americans-death-rate-covid-19-coronavirus.

22 Rebecca Nagle, "Native Americans Being Left Out of US Coronavirus Data and Labelled as 'Other,'" *The Guardian*, 24 April 2020, https://www.theguardian.com/us-news/2020/apr/24/us-native-americans-left-out-coronavirus-data.

23 Robert Samuels and Toluse Olorunnipa, *His Name Is George Floyd: One Man's Life and the Struggle for Racial Justice* (New York: Viking Press, 2022), Apple eBook.

24 Mbembe, "The Universal Right to Breathe."

25 Christian Rutz, Matthias-Claudio Loretto, Amanda E. Bates, et al., "Covid-19 Lockdown Allows Researchers to Quantify the Effects of Human Activity on Wildlife," *Nature Ecology and Evolution* 4 (September 2020): 1156.

26 Christian Rutz, "Studying Pauses and Pulses in Human Mobility and Their Environmental Impacts," *Nature Reviews: Earth & Environment* 3 (March 2022): 157.

27 Hannah Ellis-Petersen, Rebecca Ratcliffe, Sam Cowie, Joe Parkin Daniels, and Lily Kuo, "'It's Positively Alpine!': Disbelief in Big Cities as Air Pollution Falls," *The Guardian*, 11 April 2020, https://www.theguardian.com/environment/2020/apr/11/positively-alpine-disbelief-air-pollution-falls-lockdown-coronavirus.

28 John Brunton, "'Nature Is Taking Back Venice': Wildlife Returns to Tourist-Free City," *Guardian*, 20 March 2020, https://www.theguardian.com/environment/2020/mar/20/nature-is-taking-back-venice-wildlife-returns-to-tourist-free-city.

29 The Associated Press, "Virus Lockdown Gives Venice a Shot at Reimagining Tourism," CTV News, 16 May 2020, https://www.ctvnews.ca/health/coronavirus/virus-lockdown-gives-venice-a-shot-at-reimagining-tourism-1.4942444.

30 Amanda Bates, quoted in Emily Anthes, "Did Nature Heal during the Pandemic 'Anthropause'?" *New York Times*, 21 July 2022, https://www.nytimes.com/2022/07/16/science/pandemic-nature-anthropause.html.

31 Manuela López Restrepo, "'Revenge Travel' Is Surging. Here's What You Need to Know," NPR, 16 June 2022, https://www.npr.org/2022/06/16/1105323610/flight-tickets-inflation-pandemic-revenge-travel-vacation-europe-recession.

32 Nadja Popovich, Livia Albeck-Ripka, and Kendra Pierre-Louis, "The Trump Administration is Reversing Nearly 100 Environmental Rules. Here's the Full List," *New York Times*, 20 May

NOTES TO PAGES 39–47

2020, https://www.nytimes.com/interactive/2020/climate/trump-environment-rollbacks.html.

33 Ane Alencar, quoted in Ernesto Londoño, Manuela Andreoni and Letícia Casado, "Amazon Deforestation Soars as Pandemic Hobbles Enforcement," *The New York Times*, 6 June 2020, https://www.nytimes.com/2020/06/06/world/americas/amazon-deforestation-brazil.html.

34 Adriano Karipuna, quoted in ibid.

35 Judith Butler, "Capitalism Has Its Limits," *Verso blog*, 30 March 2020, https://www.versobooks.com/blogs/4603-capitalism-has-its-limits.

36 Mbembe, "The Universal Right to Breathe," S61.

Pause and Effect

1 Georges Perec, *An Attempt at Exhausting a Place in Paris*, trans. Marc Lowenthal (Cambridge: Wakefield Press, 2010), 29.

2 Gary Bettman, quoted in NHL.com, "NHL to Pause Season due to Coronavirus," NHL website, 12 March 2020, https://www.nhl.com/news/nhl-coronavirus-to-provide-update-on-concerns/c-316131734.

3 Dorinda L. Peacock and Mark P. Henriques, "Push the Pause Button? Contracts and Covid-19," *The National Law Review*, 7 April 2020, https://www.natlawreview.com/article/push-pause-button-contracts-and-covid-19.

4 Osman Dar, "Is Covid-19 an Opportunity for More Equitable Health Systems in the Middle East?" *Euro News*, 9 April 2020, https://www.euronews.com/2020/04/03/covid-19-pandemic-and-health-systems-in-the-middle-east-a-chance-for-a-new-beginning-view.

5 Lucretius, *On the Nature of Things*, trans. W.H.D. Rouse, Loeb Classical Library (Cambridge: Harvard University Press, 1982), 254–5.

6 Ibid., 260–1.

7 E.J. Kenney, *Lucretius: De Rerum Natura Book III* (Cambridge: Cambridge University Press, 1971), 197.

NOTES TO PAGES 48–55

8 David F. Bright, "The Plague and the Structure of 'De Rerum Natura,'" *Latomus* 30, no. 3 (1971): 610; 619.
9 Lucretius, *The Nature of the Universe*, trans. R.E. Latham (Harmondsworth: Penguin Books, 1961), 254.
10 See J.J. Haladyn, *The Art and Craft of Agreeing to Teach Your Course Online* (London: Blue Medium Press, 2023). This text was written in response to an invitation from my colleague Maria Belén Ordóñez and originally published in the OCADFA *Newsletter*, "Our Labour in Times of COVID-19," in Summer 2020.
11 Emily Baron Cadloff, "The Big Transition Begins as Faculty Switch to Online Learning in Response to Covid-19," *University Affairs*, 23 March 2020, https://www.universityaffairs.ca/news/news-article/the-big-experiment-begins-as-faculty-switch-to-online-learning-in-response-to-covid-19.
12 Emma Zuck, quoted in "'This Is Not Going to Be the Same': How University Students Are Coping with Covid-19 Measures," *National Post*, 9 April 2020, https://nationalpost.com/news/canada/this-is-not-going-to-be-the-same-how-university-students-are-coping-with-covid-19-measures.
13 Jiang Jiehong to Li Lin, "In Fashion at Home," in *The Otherness of the Everyday: Twelve Conversations from the Chinese Art World during the Covid-19 Pandemic*, ed. Jiang Jiehong (Bristol: Intellect, 2021), 103.
14 CBC Sports, "NHL Considering August Return without Fans: Report," *CBC News*, 6 April 2020, https://www.cbc.ca/sports/nhl-late-summer-return-discussion-1.5523339.
15 Giorgio Agamben, "The State of Exception Provoked by an Unmotivated Emergency," *Positions*, 26 February 2020, http://positionswebsite.org/giorgio-agamben-the-state-of-exception-provoked-by-an-unmotivated-emergency/.
16 Massimo Cacciari and Giorgio Agamben, "Massimo Cacciari, Giorgio Agamben – About the 'Green Pass' Decree," trans. Lena Bloch, *Medium*, 27 July 2021, https://lenabloch.medium.com/massimo-cacciari-giorgio-agamben-about-the-green-pass-decree-8a7e0ce5b066.

NOTES TO PAGES 55–61

17 Roberto Esposito to Francesco Borgonovo, "Debate on the Green Pass: Roberto Esposito," *European Journal of Psychoanalysis*, 13 October 2021, https://www.journal-psychoanalysis.eu/articles/debate-on-the-green-pass-roberto-esposito.

18 David Black, quoted in Jennifer Ferreira, "Why People Are Drawn to Covid-19 Conspiracy Theories," CTV News, 12 May 2020, https://www.ctvnews.ca/health/coronavirus/why-people-are-drawn-to-covid-19-conspiracy-theories-1.4936176.

19 Jon Allsop, "The Everything Virus: Two Years of Journalists Scrambling to Make Sense of an Ever-Changing Pandemic," *Columbia Journalism Review* (The Pandemic Issue, June 2022): pandemic.cjr.org.

20 Eliot Weinberger, "The American Virus," *London Review of Books* 42, no. 11 (June 2020): 3; 8.

21 Albert Camus, quoted in Jacqueline Rose, "'The Plague': Pointing the Finger," *London Review of Books* 42, no. 9 (May 2020): 3.

22 Eva Amsen, "Colorful Images Make the SARS-CoV-2 Virus Look Less Threatening," *Forbes*, 28 October 2021, https://www.forbes.com/sites/evaamsen/2021/10/28/colorful-images-make-the-sars-cov-2-virus-look-less-threatening.

23 David Hume, *An Enquiry concerning Human Reason* (Oxford: Oxford University Press, 2008), 21.

24 Fred Khumalo, "Let's Run the Voodoo Down!" in *Lockdown Extended: Corona Chronicles*, ed. Melinda Ferguson (Cape Town: Melinda Ferguson Books, 2020), Apple eBook.

25 Anca Anghalae, "Challenge: Storytelling in the Covid-19 Era," Youtube, 11 June 2021, https://www.youtube.com/watch?v=EQMmEGwtRMw. See also the Earth Observation Dashboard: https://www.eodashboardhackathon.org.

26 See Fang Fang, *Wuhan Diary: Dispatches from a Quarantined City*, trans. Michael Berry (Toronto: Harper Collins, 2020), Apple eBook.

27 Rose, "'The Plague': Pointing the Finger," 3.

28 Giovanni Boccaccio, *Decameron*, trans. Guido Waldman (New York: Oxford University Press, 2008), 6.

157

Seeing the Virus

1 Georges Perec, *An Attempt at Exhausting a Place in Paris*, trans. Marc Lowenthal (Cambridge: Wakefield Press, 2010), 15.

2 Penelope Ironstone, "The Pandemic Is (Extra) Ordinary," *Topia: Canadian Journal of Cultural Studies* (Covid-19 Essays, 2020): https://www.utpjournals.press/journals/topia/covid-19-essays/the-pandemic-is-extra-ordinary.

3 Rachel Ossip, "Living Inside: The Virus Comes to Visit," in *There Is No Outside: Covid-19 Dispatches*, eds. Jessie Kindig, Mark Krotov, and Marco Roth (New York: Verso, 2020), Apple ebook.

4 Ibid., 58; 54.

5 Fang Fang, *Wuhan Diary: Dispatches from a Quarantined City*, trans. Michael Berry (Toronto: Harper Collins, 2020), Apple ebook.

6 Franco "Bifo" Berardi, "Diary of the Psycho-Deflation #3: 'As If It Were Yesterday,'" *Verso Blog*, 9 April 2020, https://www.verso books.com/blogs/4655-bifo-diary-of-the-psycho-deflation-3-as-if-it-were-yesterday.

7 Afsoun Afsahi, Emily Beausoleil, Rikki Dean, Selen A. Ercan, and Jean-Paul Gagnon, "Five Lessons for Democracy from the Covid-19 Pandemic," in *The Long Year: A 2020 Reader*, eds. Thomas Sugrue and Caitlin Zaloom (New York: Columbia University Press, 2022), 386.

8 Alan Feuer and Liam Stack, "New York City Considers Temporary Graves for Virus Victims," *New York Times*, 6 April 2020, https://www.nytimes.com/2020/04/06/nyregion/mass-graves-nyc-parks-coronavirus.html.

9 Michel Ragon, *The Space of Death: A Study of Funerary Architecture, Decoration, and Urbanism*, trans. Alan Sheridan (Charlottesville: University Press of Virginia, 1983), 3–4.

10 Lucretius, *On the Nature of Things*, trans. W.H.D. Rouse, Loeb Classical Library (Cambridge: Harvard University Press, 1982), 284–5.

NOTES TO PAGES 69–78

11 Giovanni Boccaccio, *Decameron*, trans. Guido Waldman (New York: Oxford University Press, 2008), 12.

12 Fang Fang, *Wuhan Diary*.

13 Lise Josefsen Hermann, "When Bodies Piled Up: Inside Ecuador's First Coronavirus Hotspot," *Al Jazeera News*, 17 June 2020, https://www.aljazeera.com/indepth/features/bodies-piled-ecuador-covid-19-hotspot-200617142117507.html.

14 Patricia Marin Gines, quoted in ibid.

15 Colin Butler, "London's 2022 Pandemic Deaths Are on Track to Surpass All of 2021 – And It's Only July," CBC News, 28 July 2022, https://www.cbc.ca/news/toront/toront/toront-ontario-covid-deaths-1.6533791.

16 Jennifer Bieman, "Face Masks Mandatory in All London Indoor Public Places Starting Saturday," *London Free Press*, 17 July 2020, https://lfpress.com/news/local-news/masks-will-be-manda tory-in-all-indoor-public-places-across-london-starting-Saturday.

17 Catharine Arnold, *Pandemic 1918* (New York: St Martin's Press, 2018), 14.

18 Emily Baumgaertner, "Covid-19 Doctors Running Out of Masks? Try a Bandanna, the CDC Says," *Los Angeles Times*, 21 March 2020, https://www.latimes.com/politics/story/2020-03-21/coronavirus-mask-bandanna-covid-19-bandanna.

19 Laura Osman and Marie Woolf, "Some Nurses Lack Proper PPE amid Omicron Covid-19 Surge, Union Says," Global News, 14 January 2022, https://globalnews.ca/news/8510939/nurses-ppe-omicron-covid-19.

20 Alaa Elassar, "Louis Vuitton Is Releasing a Face Shield with Golden Studs to Protect Luxury Buyers from Coronavirus," CNN Style, 12 September 2020, https://www.cnn.com/style/article/louis-vuitton-face-shield-trnd/index.html.

21 Meghan Navoy, "Rosemarine Textiles in Covid-19," Rosemarine Textiles website (accessed 30 July 2020), https://www.rose marinetextiles.com/covid19.

NOTES TO PAGES 79–87

22 Peter Jüni, quoted in CBC News, "Ontario Lifts Mask Mandates in Most Spaces, But It's No 'Light Switch' for Pre-Pandemic Life, Expert Says," CBC News, 21 March 2022, https://www.cbc.ca/news/toront/toronto/covid19-ont-masks-march-21-2022-1.6385293.

23 Manuela López Restrepo, "'Revenge Travel' Is Surging. Here's What You Need to Know," NPR, 16 June 2022, https://www.npr.org/2022/06/16/1105323610/flight-tickets-inflation-pandemic-revenge-travel-vacation-europe-recession.

24 Allsop, "The Everything Virus."

25 Judith Butler, "Capitalism Has Its Limits," *Verso blog*, 30 March 2020, https://www.versobooks.com/blogs/4603-capitalism-has-its-limits.

26 Franco "Bifo" Berardi, "Beyond the Breakdown: Three Meditations on a Possible Aftermath," *e-flux Conversations*, 31 March 2020, https://conversations.e-flux.com/t/beyond-the-breakdown-three-meditations-on-a-possible-aftermath-by-franco-bifo-berardi/9727.

27 David Harvey, "Anti-Capitalist Politics in the Time of Covid-19," *Reading Marx's Capital with David Harvey*, 19 March 2020, http://davidharvey.org/2020/03/anti-capitalist-politics-in-the-time-of-covid-19.

28 Slavoj Žižek, *Pandemic! Covid-19 Shakes the World* (New York: OR Books, 2020), 39.

29 Jean-Luc Nancy, "Communovirus," trans. David Fernbach, *Verso Blog*, 27 March 2020, https://www.versobooks.com/blogs/4626-communovirus.

A Theory of Social Distancing

1 Georges Perec, *An Attempt at Exhausting a Place in Paris*, trans. Marc Lowenthal (Cambridge: Wakefield Press, 2010), 10.

2 Michel Foucault, *Discipline and Punish: The Birth of the Prison*, trans. Alan Sheridan (New York: Vintage Books, 1995), 198.

3 Slavoj Žižek, *Pandemic! Covid-19 Shakes the World* (New York: OR Books, 2020), 130.

NOTES TO PAGES 87–94

4 Albert Camus, *The Plague*, trans. Robin Buss (New York: Penguin Books, 2013), 49.

5 Centers for Disease Control and Prevention, "Social Distancing," CDC website (accessed 6 October 2020), https://www.cdc.gov/coronavirus/2019-ncov/prevent-getting-sick/social-distancing.html. Since 2023, this has been replaced with a more generic definition listed under "Prevention Actions to Add as Needed": https://www.cdc.gov/coronavirus/2019-ncov/prevent-getting-sick/prevention.html.

6 World Health Organization and China, "Report of the WHO-China Joint Mission on Coronavirus Disease 2019 (Covid-19)," WHO website, 16–24 February 2020, https://www.who.int/docs/default-source/coronaviruse/who-china-joint-mission-on-covid-19-final-report.pdf.

7 George Gao, quoted in Jon Cohen, "Not Wearing Masks to Protect against Coronavirus Is a 'Big Mistake,' Top Chinese Scientist Says," *Science*, 27 March 2020, https://www.sciencemag.org/news/2020/03/not-wearing-masks-protect-against-coronavirus-big-mistake-top-chinese-scientist-says.

8 Katie Pearce, "What Is Social Distancing and How Can It Slow the Spread of Covid-19?" *Hub*, 13 March 2020, https://hub.jhu.edu/2020/03/13/what-is-social-distancing/.

9 See #StayTheFuckHome (accessed 17 May 2020), https://staythefuckhome.com.

10 Zack Beauchamp, "Canada Succeeded on Coronavirus Where America Failed. Why?" *Vox*, 4 May 2020, https://www.vox.com/2020/5/4/21242750/coronavirus-covid-19-united-states-canada-trump-trudeau. See also Amanda Coletta, "Canada's Coronavirus Performance Hasn't Been Perfect. But It's Done Far Better Than the U.S.," *The Washington Post*, 15 July 2020, https://www.washingtonpost.com/world/the_americas/coronavirus-canada-united-states/2020/07/14/0686330a-c14c-11ea-b4f6-cb39cd8940fb_story.html.

11 Aaron Timms, "Distance Must Be Maintained," in *There Is No Outside: Covid-19 Dispatches*, eds. Jessie Kindig, Mark Krotov, and Marco Roth (New York: Verso, 2020), 206–7.

161

NOTES TO PAGES 95–9

12 Faith Karimi and Jamiel Lynch, "Young People Are Throwing Coronavirus Parties with a Payout When One Gets Infected, Official Says," CNN, 2 July 2020, https://www.cnn.com/2020/07/02/us/alabama-coronavirus-parties-trnd/index.html.

13 Josh K. Elliott, "'I Thought This Was a Hoax': Man, 30, Dies After Texas 'Covid Party,'" Global News, 13 July 2020, https://globalnews.ca/news/7169518/coronavirus-covid-party-death-hoax/.

14 Giorgio Agamben, "The State of Exception Provoked by an Unmotivated Emergency," Positions, 26 February 2020, http://positionswebsite.org/giorgio-agamben-the-state-of-exception-provoked-by-an-unmotivated-emergency/.

15 Giorgio Agamben, "Clarifications," 17 March 2020, in "Coronavirus and Philosophers: A Tribune," special issue of European Journal of Psychoanalysis (February–May 2020): https://www.journal-psychoanalysis.eu/articles/coronavirus-and-philosophers/.

16 Giorgio Agamben, "Social Distancing," in Where Are We Now? The Epidemic as Politics, trans. Valeria Dani (London: Eris, 2021), 32.

17 Benjamin Bratton, The Revenge of the Real: Politics for a Post-Pandemic World (New York: Verso, 2021), 57.

18 Thomas Brauch, Ellie Brocklehurst, Sarah Hess and Ingrid Volkmer, "Social Media & Covid-19: A Global Study of Digital Crisis Interaction among Gen Z and Millennials," WHO website, 1 December 2021, https://www.who.int/news-room/feature-stories/detail/social-media-covid-19-a-global-study-of-digital-crisis-interaction-among-gen-z-and-millennials.

19 Caleb Carr and Rebecca Hayes, "Social Media: Defining, Developing, and Divining," Atlantic Journal of Communication 23, no. 46–65 (2015): 50.

20 Mayo Clinic, "Here Is Today's Covid-19 Vaccine Myth Buster," Facebook, 13 December 2020, https://m.facebook.com/MayoClinic/photos/a.375657867516/10157487028027517/?type=3&p=90&_se_imp=19RPDroFr8ifgljGW.

NOTES TO PAGES 100–6

21 Nexstar Media Wire, "20% of Americans Believe Government Is Injecting Microchips in Covid-19 Vaccines, Survey Finds," Fox8 News, 19 July 2021, https://fox8.com/news/coronavirus/20-of-americans-believe-government-is-injecting-microchips-in-covid-19-vaccines-survey-finds.

22 Brenda K. Wiederhold, "Social Media Use During Social Distancing," *Cyberpsychology, behavior, and Social Networking* 23, no. 5 (2020): 1.

23 World Health Organization. "Novel Coronavirus (2019-nCov): Situation Report – 13," WHO website, 2 February 2020, https://www.who.int/docs/default-source/coronaviruse/situation-reports/20200202-sitrep-13-ncov-v3.pdf.

24 Isabelle MacNeil, "Why There Are No Microchips in the Covid-19 Vaccine," CBC Kids News, 4 October 2021, https://www.cbc.ca/kidsnews/post/watch-why-there-are-no-microchips-in-the-covid-19-vaccine.

25 Hannah Arendt, *The Human Condition* (Chicago: The University of Chicago Press, 1998), 28.

26 Charles B. Stone, Li Guan, Gabriella LaBarbera, Melissa Ceren, Brandon Garcia, Kelly Huie, Carissa Stump, and Qi Wang, "Why Do People Share Memories Online? An Examination of the Motives and Characteristics of Social Media Users," *Memory* (2022): https://doi.org/10.1080/09658211.2022.2040534.

27 Alice Marwick and danah boyd, "Networked Privacy: How Teenagers Negotiate Context in Social Media," *New Media & Society* 16, no. 7 (2014): 1016.

28 Tong King Lee and Dingkun Wang, "Introduction: Translation in the Time of #COVID-19," *Translation and Social Media Communication in the Age of the Pandemic* (London: Routledge, 2022), 1.

29 Jiang Jiehong to Xiang Biao, "The State of Suspension: Conversation with Xiang Biao, 6 June 2020," in *The Otherness of the Everyday: Twelve Conversations from the Chinese Art World during the Covid-19 Pandemic*, ed. Jiang Jiehong (Bristol: Intellect, 2021), 19–21.

NOTES TO PAGES 106–14

30 Xiang Biao to Jiang Jiehong, in ibid., 22.
31 Giorgio Agamben to Dimitra Pouliopoulou, "Polemos Epidemios: Interview," in Agamben, *Where Are We Now?*, 61.

Asynchronicity

1 Georges Perec, *An Attempt at Exhausting a Place in Paris*, trans. Marc Lowenthal (Cambridge: Wakefield Press, 2010), 9.
2 Albert Camus, *The Plague*, trans. Laura Marris (New York: Vintage Books, 2022), 7.
3 Annika Mann, *Reading Contagion: The Hazards of Reading in the Age of Print* (Charlottesville: University of Virginia Press, 2018), 13.
4 Miranda [Leduc], "Four Ways That Reading Can Save Your Sanity during Covid-19," Medicine Hat Public Library blog, 31 March 2020, https://mhpl.shortgrass.ca/blog/reading-save-your-sanity.
5 Marcello Giovanelli, quoted in Stephanie Hogan, "Our Reading Habits Changed with Pandemic Lockdowns – Here's How," CBC Radio, 28 December 2021, https://www.cbc.ca/radio/Sunday/the-Sunday-magazine-for-october-31-2021-1.6229995/our-reading-habits-changed-with-pandemic-lockdowns-here-s-how-1.6252564.
6 Katrin Rupp, "The Consolation of Literature: Reading Giovanni Boccaccio's *Decameron* during the Covid-19 Pandemic," *New Chaucer Studies: Pedagogy and Profession* 2.2 (Autumn 2021): 77.
7 Elisabeth Stelson, "Covid and Camus: Reflections on *The Plague*, Collective Experience, and Qualitative Inquiry during a Pandemic," *Qualitative Social Work* 20, nos. 1–2 (2021): 42.
8 Franco "Bifo" Berardi, "Diary of the Psycho-Deflation #2: 'Normality Must Not Return,'" *Verso Blog*, 6 April 2020, https://www.versobooks.com/blogs/4640-bifo-diary-of-the-psycho-deflation-2-normality-must-not-return.
9 Jhumpa Lahiri, *Translating Myself and Others* (Princeton: Princeton University Press, 2022), 100.

164

NOTES TO PAGES 115–22

10　Camus, *The Plague*, trans. Marris, 7.

11　Hogan, "Our Reading Habits Changed."

12　Kaitlin Pomerantz, "Teaching Art Online under Covid-19," *Hyperallergic*, 17 March 2020, https://hyperallergic.com/547986/teaching-art-online-under-covid-19.

13　Angela Minichiello, Oenardi Lawanto, Wade Goodridge, Assad Iqbal, and Muhammad Asghar, "Flipping the Digital Switch: Affective Responses of STEM Undergraduates to Emergency Remote Teaching during the Covid-19 Pandemic," *Project Leadership and Society* 3 (December 2022): https://doi.org/10.1016/j.plas.2022.100043.

14　Charles Hodges, Stephanie Moore, Barb Lockee, Torrey Trust, and Aaron Bond, "The Difference between Emergency Remote Teaching and Online Learning," *Educause Review*, 27 March 2020, https://er.educause.edu/articles/2020/3/the-difference-between-emergency-remote-teaching-and-online-learning.

15　Shawn Micallef, "Covid-19 Proves to Be a Learning Experience for Universities," *The Star*, 18 March 2020, https://www.thestar.com/opinion/contributors/2020/03/18/covid-19-proves-to-be-a-learning-experience-for-universities.html.

16　Precademics 85.42.1, "On Pause: Academic Precarity in the Covid-19 Era and Beyond in Greece," *European Journal of Turkish Studies* 30 (2020): 7.

17　Jiang Jiehong to Xiang Biao, "The State of Suspension: Conversation with Xiang Biao, 6 June 2020," in *The Otherness of the Everyday: Twelve Conversations from the Chinese Art World during the Covid-19 Pandemic*, ed. Jiang Jiehong (Bristol: Intellect, 2021), 26.

18　Elizabeth Outka, *Viral Modernism: The Influenza Pandemic and Interwar Literature* (New York: Columbia University Press, 2020), 15.

19　Claire Ballentine and Allison McNeely, "Employees Are Returning to the Office, Just to Sit on Zoom Calls," *Bloomberg*, 1 April 2022, https://www.bloomberg.com/news/articles/2022-04-01/employees-are-returning-to-office-post-covid-just-to-sit-on-zoom-calls.

NOTES TO PAGES 123–31

20 Samual Amponsah, Micheal M. van Wyk and Michael Kojo Kolugu, "Academic Experiences of 'Zoom-Fatigue' as a Virtual Streaming Phenomenon during the Covid-19 Pandemic," *International Journal of Web-Based Learning and Teaching Technologies* 17, no. 6 (2022): 12, 7.

21 Ibid., 12.

22 Bifo, "Diary of the Psycho-Deflation #2."

23 Stephen Burgen, "Spain Plans 'Digital Nomad' Visa Scheme to Attract Remote Workers," *The Guardian*, 25 September 2022, https://www.theguardian.com/world/2022/sep/25/spain-plans-digital-nomad-visa-scheme-to-attract-remote-workers.

24 *Bangkok Post*, "Malaysia Rolls Out Digital Nomad Visa. Malaysia Aims to Become Southeast Asia's Remote Work Hub," 21 September 2022, https://www.bangkokpost.com/business/2396855/malaysias-new-digital-nomad-visa-aims-to-make-it-southeast-asias-remote-work-hub-but-competition-from-bali-is-fierce.

25 Bifo, "Beyond the Breakdown."

26 Benjamin Bratton, *The Revenge of the Real: Politics for a Post-Pandemic World* (New York: Verso, 2021), 89.

27 Elizabeth Outka, "The Pandemic Has Given Us a Bad Case of Narrative Vertigo. Literature Can Help," *The Washington Post*, 25 January 2022, https://www.washingtonpost.com/outlook/2022/01/25/narrative-vertigo-woolf-yeats-pandemic-literature.

On Abstraction, Boredom, and Pausing

1 Georges Perec, *An Attempt at Exhausting a Place in Paris*, trans. Marc Lowenthal (Cambridge: Wakefield Press, 2010), 21.

2 Roger Quilliot, *The Sea and Prisons: A Commentary on the Life and Works of Albert Camus*, trans. Emmett Parker (Alabama: University of Alabama Press, 1970), 150, 136.

3 Albert Camus, *The Plague*, trans. Laura Marris (New York: Vintage Books, 2022), 68.

4 Perec, *An Attempt at Exhausting a Place in Paris*, 29.

5 Camus, *The Plague*, trans. Marris, 96.

NOTES TO PAGES 132–6

6 Franco "Bifo" Berardi, "Diary of the Psycho-Deflation," *Verso Blog*, 18 March 2020, https://www.versobooks.com/blogs/4600-bifo-diary-of-the-psycho-deflation.

7 Bifo to Andreas Petrossiants, "Franco 'Bifo' Berardi: Pandemic and the Reset of the Global Machine," *Strelka Mag*, 6 May 2020, https://strelkamag.com/en/article/franco-bifo-berardi-pandemic-and-the-reset-of-the-global-machine.

8 Franco "Bifo" Berardi, "Resign," *e-flux* 124 (February 2022): https://www.e-flux.com/journal/124/443422/resign.

9 Plurinational and Popular Women's Parliament and the Feminist Organisations of Ecuador, "Care For the People in Times of Pandemic: Collective Reflections to Overcome Uncertainty, Essays to Avoid Inhabiting Impotence," trans. Hans Bryssinck, *SPIN* blog, 20 April 2020, https://www.spinspin.be/blog/care-for-the-people-in-times-of-pandemic-collective-reflections-to-overcome-uncertainty-essays-to-avoid-inhabiting-impotence.

10 Ibid.

11 Maya Wilson-Sanchez, "Replicas and Reunions: Ancient and Contemporary Ceramics from Ecuador," exhibition description on Gardiner Museum website (accessed 14 November 2022): https://www.gardinermuseum.on.ca/event/replicas-and-reunions-ancient-and-contemporary-ceramics-from-ecuador.

12 Magda Sawon, "How to Experience 'Experience Art' in a Pandemic – A Modest Proposal," press release, reprinted in *Left Is Right, Down Is Up: Serkan Özkaya and Joseph Beuys* (exhibition catalogue) (Postmasters Gallery, n.d. [circa 2021]), n.p.

13 Jason Farago, "Now Virtual and in Video, Museum Websites Shake Off the Dust," *New York Times*, 23 April 2020, https://www.nytimes.com/2020/04/23/arts/design/best-virtual-museum-guides.html.

14 Bifo, "Diary of the Psycho-Deflation."

15 Brendan Morrow, "Pope Francis Offers Coronavirus Prayer from a Strikingly Empty St Peter's Square," *The Week*, 27 March 2020, https://theweek.com/speedreads/905396/pope-francis-offers-coronavirus-prayer-from-strikingly-empty-st-peters-square.

NOTES TO PAGES 137–43

16 Zhu Zheqin to Jiang Jiehong, "The Un-isolatable: Conversation with Zhu Zheqin, 12 September 2020," in *The Otherness of the Everyday: Twelve Conversations from the Chinese Art World during the Covid-19 Pandemic*, ed. Jiang Jiehong (Bristol: Intellect, 2021), 192.

17 Steven Ellis, "What It's Like Watching an NHL Game without Fans," *The Hockey News*, 6 January 2022, https://thehockey news.com/news/what-its-like-watching-an-nhl-game-without-fans.

18 Pi Li to Jiang Jiehong, "The End of the Museums: Conversation with Pi Li, 20 June 2020," *The Otherness of the Everyday*, 54.

19 Andrew Dickson, "You Can't Visit the Museum, but Your Robot Can," *New York Times*, 15 April 2020, https://www.nytimes.com/2020/04/15/arts/museums-robots-coronavirus.html.

20 Jiang Jiehong to Pi Li, "The End of the Museums," in *The Otherness of the Everyday*, 56–7.

21 David Black, quoted in Jennifer Ferreira, "Why People Are Drawn to Covid-19 Conspiracy Theories," CTV News, 12 May 2020, https://www.ctvnews.ca/health/coronavirus/why-people-are-drawn-to-covid-19-conspiracy-theories-1.4936176.

22 Andrew K. Przybylski, Kou Murayama, Cody R. DeHaan, and Valerie Gladwell, "Motivational, Emotional, and Behavioral Correlates of Fear of Missing Out," *Computers in Human Behavior* 29, no. 4 (July 2013): https://doi.org/10.1016/j.chb.2013.02.014.

23 Darshina Dhunnoo, quoted in "'This Is Not Going to Be the Same': How University Students Are Coping with Covid-19 Measures," *National Post*, 9 April 2020, https://nationalpost.com/news/canada/this-is-not-going-to-be-the-same-how-university-students-are-coping-with-covid-19-measures.

24 Richard A. Friedman, "Is the Lockdown Making You Depressed, or Are You Just Bored?," *New York Times*, 21 August 2020, https://www.nytimes.com/2020/08/21/opinion/sunday/covid-depression-boredom.html.

NOTES TO PAGES 143–7

25 Adam Grant, "We're Living through the 'Boring Apocalypse',"
   The New York Times, 10 December 2021, https://www.nytimes.
   com/2021/12/10/opinion/covid-omicron-psychology-fear.html.

26 Fang Fang, *Wuhan Diary: Dispatches from a Quarantined City*,
   trans. Michael Berry (Toronto: Harper Collins, 2020), Apple
   ebook.

27 Marris and Kaplan, *States of Plague: Reading Albert Camus in a
   Pandemic*, 37.

28 Camus, *The Plague*, trans. Marris, 196.

29 Stephen M. Kissler, Christine Tedijanto, Edward Goldstein,
   Yonatan H. Grad, and Marc Lipsitch, "Projecting the Transmission Dynamics of SARS-CoV-2 through the Postpandemic
   Period," *Science* 368, no. 6493 (22 May 2020), https://science.
   sciencemag.org/content/368/6493/860.

30 Anurag Agrawal, quoted in Teena Thacker, "Pandemic Headed
   for a Long Pause, but Not the End, Warn Experts," *The Economic Times*, 26 January 2022, https://economictimes.india
   times.com/news/india/pandemic-headed-for-a-long-pause-
   but-not-the-end-warn-experts/articleshow/89127872.cms.

31 Kim Wong-Shing, "When Covid-19 Is No Longer a Pandemic:
   How Our Reality Changes," *CNET*, 28 December 2021, https://
   www.cnet.com/health/when-covid-19-is-no-longer-a-pan
   demic-how-our-reality-changes.

32 Elizabeth Outka, "The Pandemic Has Given Us a Bad Case of
   Narrative Vertigo. Literature Can Help," *The Washington Post*,
   25 January 2022, https://www.washingtonpost.com/outlook/
   2022/01/25/narrative-vertigo-woolf-yeats-pandemic-literature.

Index

2020 (year), xiv, 17, 27, 33, 34, 36, 52, 53, 61, 64, 67, 68, 69, 70, 76, 83, 84, 89, 91, 105, 106, 116, 136, 145
2021 (year), xv, 24, 54, 67, 72, 87, 99, 107, 146
2022 (year), xi, xv, 29, 38, 41, 45, 56, 71, 76, 79, 80, 82, 83, 84, 88, 92, 107, 108, 116, 120, 122, 129, 136, 140
2023 (year), xi, xii, 65, 107, 119, 129, 142, 146

Abdullah, Melina, 32
Agamben, Giorgio, xiii, 13, 16–17, 54, 95, 107; Italian National Research Council, 16
Alencar, Amazônia Ane, 39
Alter, Alexandra, 13
Amponsah, Samuel, 123
animals, 36–7
anthropause, 30, 34–8, 38, 41; and anthrosurge, 38
Arendt, Hannah, 102

Beuys, Joseph, 3
Biao, Xiang, 106

Bifo, 67, 81, 113, 124, 126, 132–3, 134, 136
Black, David, 55, 141
Black Lives Matter, 32
Blackman, Francis, 12
Black Plague, 25
Boccaccio, Giovanni, 69; *Decameron*, 11, 61–2, 112–13
Bogoch, Dr Isaac, xi
book reading, 111–12, 115
boredom: Covid-19, 141–4; Camus, 144; depression, 143; Fang Fang, 144
Bratton, Benjamin: *The Revenge of the Real*, 146
Brazilian environmental policy, 39–40
breathing, 27–8, 30, 40, 41; George Floyd, 34; as a human right, 29–30, 34
Breton, André, 74
Burgen, Stephen, 125
Butler, Judith, xiii, 17, 40, 81

Camus, Albert, 20, 133; Covid-19, 19, 61, 110; *The Plague*, 18–19, 56, 87, 113, 114–15, 129, 130, 131, 144, 145, 147
Canada, 36, 71, 73, 76, 84, 92

INDEX

Canadian Federation of Nurses, 76
capitalism, xiii, 40, 81, 82–3, 96, 134
Carr, Caleb, and Rebecca Hayes, 97
Center for Disease Control (CDC),
88–9
Cevallos, Pamela, 134
China, xi, 7, 16, 89, 91
Cobb, Jelani, 31
conspiracy theories, 55, 95, 141
Covid-19: ambiguity, 147; books on,
109; boredom, 141–4; and breathing,
28–9; capitalism, 81–3, 132, 134; ca-
sualties from, 22; collapse, 132; effects, xii; first-hand narratives, 12,
19; the future of, 145–6; government
actions, 22, 38, 39, 67, 89; and the
healthcare system, 66; images from,
83–4, 136; imagination, 17, 20; the
imagined, 62, 147; inequalities, 82;
the knowable, 26–7; memes, xiv–xv;
news consumption, 80; as pandemic, 22; as pause, xiv; popular
media, 23–4; psychology, 66; race,
32–4, 39–42, 68; sci-fi, 66; the social
body, 132–3; splitting of reality, 71;
symptoms, 22, 27, 66; TV, 140–1; as
unimaginable, 56–7, 63, 119; in the
US, 17, 56; utopian thought, 82;
writing, 13, 14, 15, 18. *See also* pandemic; virus
Covid parties, 95
Cummins, Eleanor, 147

Dar, Osman, 44
Deadwood "Plague" episode, 62
death, 12–13, 17; from Covid-19, 65, 67;
Lucretius, 47–9; rates in the US, 92;
treatment of the dead body, 68–70

Defoe, Daniel: *A Journal of the Plague
Year*, 11
digital work, 125
"digital Zoom revolution," 123
disaster films, 83–4
Duchamp, Marcel, 28; and *Paris Air*,
21, 23

Ecuador, 70, 133, 134
everyday life, 7, 45, 46, 52, 63–5, 91, 121,
130

face masks, 72; in Canada, 76, 79, 84;
consumerism, 78; mandates, 24, 72,
75, 79, 80, 87, 107, 134, 145; the "mask
economy," 76–8; nurses, 76; in Ontario, 72; the pause, 80; policy in
Canada, 134; policies, 79, 90, 107;
purpose of, 72; shortages, 75–6;
Spanish flu, 72–4; as surreal, 74–5,
76, 78; in the US, 76; in Wuhan,
China, 76
Fang Fang, 13, 15–16, 60–1, 67, 70, 97,
143; Wuhan, China, 15–16; Wuhan
Diary, 66
Farago, Jason, 135
fear of missing out (FOMO), 141; the
pandemic, 141; social media, 141
Floyd, George, 30–4, 40; and protests,
32
Foucault, Michel, 86

Gramsci, Antonio: *Letters from Prison*,
114
Great Plague of London, 11

Han, Byung-Chul, xiii
Hastings Contemporary, 138

172

INDEX

Hopkins, David, 21
Hume, David, 26, 59

Ironstone, Penelope, 64; and Greg
  Bird, 14
Italy, 16, 17, 36, 54–5, 87, 136

Jahangir, Alex, 17
Jiehong, Jiang, 140; and Xiang Biao,
  120

Kaplan, Alice, and Laura Marris, 17, 19
Khumalo, Fred, 24, 59–60
Klein, Naomi, xiii

Lahiri, Jhumpa, 114
Lau, Yam, 28; *Covid Life*, 130–1, 137
LaVoye, Lutiant, 12
Lee, Tong King, and Dingkun Way,
  104
lockdown, xii, xiv; contagion, 9, 10;
  protests, 56; public space, 83, 84,
  105, 136; quarantine, 8–9, 11–12;
  writing, 8–9. *See also* Covid-19;
  pandemic
Lockdown Library Project, 112
London, Ontario, 71–2
Longair, Elyse, and Jevi Peters, 139
López Restrepo, Manuela, 80
Lucretius, 69; *On the Nature of
  Things*, 10, 46–9

Malabou, Catherine, 8–9, 110–11, 114
Mann, Annika, 111
Marris, Laura, 144
Maryam, St Zena, 11
Mayo Clinic, 99
Mbembe, Achille, 29–31, 34, 40, 41

McLemee, Scott, 17
McMillen, Christian W., 9
Mead, Richard: *A Discourse on the
  Plague*, 11
Micallef, Shawn, 119
Musk, Elon, 101

Nagle, Rebecca, 33
Nancy, Jean-Luc, xiii, 82
narrative vertigo, 147
National Hockey League, 42, 53
Newton, Isaac, 11, 122
New York City, 31, 68, 69, 94

Outka, Elizabeth, 121, 127, 147
Özkaya, Serkan, 3, 135

pandemic: as abstraction, 132, 137, 145;
  art, 23, 135; art exhibits, 43, 138–40;
  asynchronous experience, 111, 116,
  119, 124, 126, 127; change, 130; choice,
  30; emptiness, 136–7, 140; endemic,
  xi; the end of, xii, xiv, 24, 80, 126,
  130, 145–7; the environment, 34–6;
  fear, 133; and historical accounts, 61;
  as imagined, xi, xiii, 20, 56, 133, 147;
  international cities, 36–7; literature,
  61; paralysis, 133; performances,
  136–7; postponed decisions, 142;
  sense of time, xi; suffocation, 31, 40;
  as surreal, 85, 92, 136, 145; uncertainty, xi, xv, 7, 46, 145, 146; as
  unimaginable, 129; work, 122. *See
  also* Covid-19
pause, xiv, xv–xvi, 5–6, 9–11, 18, 43,
  46, 63; action, 129; capitalism, 83;
  care, 134; cessation, 49; in China, 7;
  contradiction, 45–6; as a crisis of

173

INDEX

imagination, 132; defined, xi; and denial, 54–5, 68; effects of, 7; as everyday experience, 7, 45, 46, 54, 59, 83, 84, 91, 97, 130; experience of time, 127–8; feeling, 52, 53; as great pause, 146; as imagined, 51; impossibility, 147; law, 44; as long pause, 146; and opportunity for change, 44–5; popular media, 6; teaching, 50–2, 119, 124; unpause, 79, 107, 135, 142; and *vitai pausa*, 47; within a pause, 132, 146. *See also* pause button

pause button, 43–4, 51, 67, 80, 135

Pearce, Katie, 91

Perec, Georges: *An Attempt at Exhausting a Place in Paris*, 130

Plurinational and Popular Women's Parliament and the Feminist Organisations of Ecuador, 133

Pope Francis, 136

post-pandemic moment, 80, 146; and the media, 80; and international travel, 80

Procopius, 10, 17, 18

protests, 32, 56, 67, 92

quarantine, 8, 9, 11, 37, 90, 110, 121, 132

reading, 109–15

relational paralysis, 132–5. *See also* Bifo

Report of the who-China Joint Mission on Coronavirus Disease 2019, 89–90

revenge travel, 38, 80

Ricco, John Paul, 14

Rogers, Melvin L., 32

Rose, Jacqueline, 20, 61

Rousseau, Jean-Jacques, 8

Rutz, Christian, 35, 38

Samuels, Robert, and Toluse Olorunnipa, 33

Sawon, Magda, 4–5, 135

Self-Quarantine Manifesto, 91

social distancing: Centers for Disease Control and Prevention (cdc), 88–9; in China, 90–1; compliance, 92–5, 101; defined, 88; end of, 145; everyday life, 105–6; inconsistencies in, 106–7; individual freedom, 96, 101; in New York City, 94; as practice, 88, 91, 106; strategy, 90–1; theorized, 108

social media, 14, 97–103, 141; advertising oneself, 103; everyday life, 106; Facebook, 100; "infodemic," 101; misinformation, 97–101; public/private experience, 103–4; social distancing, 103–5; social life, 102, 105; teenagers, 103

Spanish flu, 12–13, 21–2, 23–6, 65, 72–4; and everyday life, 121–2

storytelling, 59–60

Thacker, Teena, 145

Thucydides, 48; *The Peloponnesian War*, 10

Toronto, 23, 50, 71, 72, 79

Trump, Donald, 55–6, 68

Trump, Eric, 56

Uffizi, the, 138, 139

United States, 17, 31, 92

university life, 87–8; students, 142; teaching, 116–23, 126–7

US environmental policy, 38–9

INDEX

virus, xi, 56, 66, 72, 82, 141, 145; Bifo, 132; death from, 68, 72; denial, 54, 80, 95, 101; in Ecuador, 70; effects of, xiv, xv, 132; Fang Fang, 60–1; 66, 67; as imagined, 57–8; invisibility, 65, 72, 79; in the news, 141; in New York City, 68; paralysis, 132–3; pause button, 80; and seeing, 65–7, 71, 72, 74; social distancing, 91; spread of, 4, 22, 28, 50, 62, 65, 70, 91, 92, 102, 107, 121, 140; symptoms, 22, 27, 66; as surreal, 66, 81, 92; and variants, 146

Weibo, Sina, 13
Wilson-Sánchez, Maya, 134
Wong-Shing, Kim, 146
World Health Organization, 14
Wright, Teresa, xi

Zheqin, Zhu, 136
Žižek, Slavoj, xiii, 13, 14, 82, 87
Zoom, 120; events, 124; fatigue, 123; revolution, 123